JOSEPH SMITH'S
COMMENTARY ON THE BIBLE

JOSEPH SMITH'S COMMENTARY ON THE BIBLE

Compiled and edited
by Kent P. Jackson

Deseret Book Company
Salt Lake City, Utah

Library of Congress Cataloging-in-Publication Data

Smith, Joseph, 1805–1844.
    Joseph Smith's commentary on the Bible / compiled and edited by Kent P. Jackson.
        p.   cm.
    Includes bibliographical references and index.
    ISBN 0–87579–903–5
    1. Bible—Commentaries. I. Jackson, Kent P. II. Title.
III. Title: Commentary on the Bible.
BX8630.S65   1994
289.3'2—dc20   94–12160
                                                              CIP

Printed in the United States of America

10 9 8 7 6 5 4 3 2 1

*To the honored memory of Martha Jane Coray, James Burgess,
Thomas Bullock, William Clayton, Wilford Woodruff,
Willard Richards, and all others who sought
to bless the world by recording the
words of the Prophet Joseph Smith*

Contents

Introduction

This book is a compilation of excerpts from Joseph Smith's discourses and writings in which he gave commentary on passages from the Bible. It collects the statements in which he discussed, analyzed, or drew significant application from biblical verses, thus shedding light on the words of earlier prophets.

History will show that the Prophet Joseph Smith was the greatest doctrinal teacher since Jesus Christ. He had a clearer understanding of truth than any other man of modern times has had, the result of much experience, over many years, with the divine source of all truth and understanding. Not only was it his mission to know but it was also his mission to teach what he knew. "It is my duty to teach the doctrine," he stated,[1] and "it is my meditation all the day, and more than my meat and drink, to know how I shall make the Saints of God to comprehend the visions that roll like an overflowing surge before my mind."[2]

---

[1]Discourse of 8 April 1844, recorded by William Clayton; Andrew F. Ehat and Lyndon W. Cook, eds., *The Words of Joseph Smith: The Contemporary Accounts of the Nauvoo Discourses of the Prophet Joseph* (Orem, Utah: Grandin Book, 1991), 363; hereafter cited as *WJS.*

[2]Discourse of 16 April 1843, recorded by Willard Richards; *WJS,* 196.

Accordingly, the record of his life shows that he dedicated himself to preaching, writing, and explaining, in informal and formal settings, what had been revealed to him from the heavens.

Much of the Prophet's teaching focused on passages from the Bible, which was frequently his tool for explaining doctrine. A typical doctrinal sermon or newspaper editorial would deal with about a dozen passages, some only cited to demonstrate a point, but others discussed and analyzed in enlightening detail.

But the Bible was not the source for Joseph Smith's theology. Revelation from God was. It is clear from his own words that he knew that what had been revealed to him was a superior source of knowledge than what he found printed on the pages of the Bible. This assertion may seem strange to those who do not know the history of the transmission of the biblical text or who do not share the testimony of the divinity of Joseph Smith's calling. But those who recognize him as God's prophet, sent to restore truth in its purity for the last days, understand that the light and knowledge that he restored is the standard against which *all* other religious ideas, traditions, or texts are to be judged.

From Joseph Smith we learn that the Bible did not arrive in the modern world without omissions and inaccuracies. He stated in his history that "many important points touching the salvation of man had been taken from the Bible, or lost before it was compiled."[3] He said he believed the Bible "as it ought to be, as it came from the pen of the original writers,"[4] or "as far as it is translated correctly" (Articles of Faith 1:8), with "translated" seemingly referring to the entire process of transmission from original manuscripts to modern-language translations. But

---

[3]1839 History; Dean C. Jessee, ed., *The Papers of Joseph Smith, Vol. 1: Autobiographical and Historical Writings* (Salt Lake City: Deseret Book, 1989), 1:372; hereafter cited as *PJS*.

[4]Discourse of 15 October 1843, recorded by Willard Richards; *WJS*, 256.

"ignorant translators, careless transcribers, or designing and corrupt priests have committed many errors."[5]

The Prophet's commission included the restoration of religious truth that had been lost through those and other processes. Much of that restoration was accomplished through the revelation of new scripture. Joseph Smith added more to the canon than any other individual known to history. The Book of Mormon, the Doctrine and Covenants, the Pearl of Great Price, and the Joseph Smith Translation draw back the windows of heaven and flood the world with gospel light as never before.

Joseph Smith's sermons and writings are also a source of revelation to the world, particularly those that open to our minds the meaning of the scriptures by correcting, explaining, and expounding on the Bible. "God may correct the scripture by me if he choose," the Prophet taught.[6] He said of the Bible, "I have the oldest book in the world and the Holy Ghost. I thank God for the old book, but more for the Holy Ghost."[7] Through the Prophet's inspired commentary on the Bible, we can see the ancient scriptures in a new light and understand them in ways that would be impossible without divine tutoring. Joseph Smith, the great seer, had the capacity to see on Bible pages things that were not visible to the natural eye. That was possible because the Spirit that animated his interpretive powers was the same Spirit that had revealed the words originally through his ancient prophetic colleagues.

By the power of the Holy Ghost, the Prophet "understood the

---

[5]Joseph Smith, *History of The Church of Jesus Christ of Latter-day Saints,* ed. B. H. Roberts, 2d ed. rev., 7 vols. (Salt Lake City: Deseret Book, 1957), 6:57.

[6]Discourse of 13 April 1843, recorded by Willard Richards; *WJS,* 191.

[7]Discourse of 7 April 1844, recorded by Wilford Woodruff; Donald Q. Cannon and Larry E. Dahl, eds., *The Prophet Joseph Smith's King Follett Discourse: A Six-Column Comparison of Original Notes and Amalgamations* (Provo, Utah: Religious Studies Center, Brigham Young University, 1983), 40.

fulness of the gospel from beginning to end, and could teach it."[8] And because he had that power, we can indeed trust his teachings to lead us in the way of salvation. "When did I ever teach anything wrong from this stand?" he asked. "I never told you I was perfect, but there is no error in the revelations which I have taught."[9] "The doctrine I teach is true."[10]

---

[8]Discourse of 11 June 1843, recorded by Levi Richards; *WJS,* 215.

[9]Discourse of 12 May 1844, recorded by Thomas Bullock; *WJS,* 369.

[10]Letter to William Smith, 18 December 1835; *PJS,* 1:175.

Concerning the Texts

The recorded words of Joseph Smith are preserved in a variety of sources. Most of his scriptural teaching is found in handwritten transcripts of sermons made by official and unofficial scribes. Newspaper editorials, journal entries, histories, and letters make up other important categories. Many of those early documents were compiled during and after the Prophet's lifetime and are now in edited form in the seven-volume *History of the Church,* edited by Elder B. H. Roberts.[1] Elder Joseph Fielding Smith's compilation, *Teachings of the Prophet Joseph Smith,*[2] contains most of the major doctrinal teachings from the *History of the Church.* The present work draws on the original documents from which those books were compiled and includes other original documents published unedited in Ehat and Cook, *The Words of Joseph Smith,*[3] and in Jessee, *The Personal Writings of*

---

[1]Joseph Smith, *History of The Church of Jesus Christ of Latter-day Saints,* ed. B. H. Roberts, 2d ed. rev., 7 vols. (Salt Lake City: Deseret Book, 1957).

[2]Joseph Smith, *Teachings of the Prophet Joseph Smith,* sel. Joseph Fielding Smith (Salt Lake City: Deseret Book, 1938).

[3]Andrew F. Ehat and Lyndon W. Cook, eds., *The Words of Joseph Smith: The Contemporary Accounts of the Nauvoo Discourses of the Prophet Joseph* (Orem, Utah: Grandin Book, 1991).

Joseph Smith[4] and *The Papers of Joseph Smith.*[5] Permission to reproduce selected texts from these sources is gratefully acknowledged.

Where multiple scribal transcripts exist for a given sermon, I have included the relevant passages from *all* of the reports, without attempting to amalgamate the sources or select one as superior. From works printed during the Prophet's lifetime, mainly newspaper editorials, I have included everything published in his name, including messages from the First Presidency. It is not certain where or to what extent the Prophet may have used the assistance of other writers when preparing items for publication. It seems safe to assume that he considered as his own, as I do in this collection, anything written or published both under his direction and over his signature.[6]

In this volume I have collected the available Bible commentary in these divers primary sources. The editing has been done to preserve the original words of the Prophet while presenting them, for the benefit of modern readers, with modern spelling and punctuation. It should be recalled that most of the material that has survived from Joseph Smith exists in "rough draft" form, unless it was published during his lifetime. Thus the editing in this collection presents the Prophet's words in a final, polished form. Because I realize that to change spelling or punctuation is to overlay a modern shading onto the original documents, I have provided references in the footnotes for those who desire to study the texts in their original form in the primary sources.

---

[4]Dean C. Jessee, ed., *The Personal Writings of Joseph Smith* (Salt Lake City: Deseret Book, 1984).

[5]Dean C. Jessee, ed., *The Papers of Joseph Smith, Vol. 1: Autobiographical and Historical Writings* (Salt Lake City: Deseret Book, 1989); *Vol. 2: Journal, 1832–1842* (Salt Lake City: Deseret Book, 1992); *Vol. 3: Journal, 1842–1844* (Salt Lake City: Deseret Book, 1995).

[6]See Joseph Smith, "To Subscribers," *Times and Seasons,* 15 March 1842, 710.

The editing of texts has been done according to the following guidelines:

Punctuation, spelling, capitalization, and grammar[7] have been modernized to conform with current usage.

Obvious scribal errors, such as inadvertent double negatives, have been deleted without ellipses.

Brackets have been used to mark the insertion of words not in the originals.

Unless grammatically or contextually necessary, scripture quoted within passages of commentary has been omitted without ellipses. Where necessary, words have been added to complete the passages of scripture that were abbreviated by scribes.

In a few places, words of the Prophet preserved by scribes in indirect discourse have been changed to direct discourse.

In a series, *and* has been replaced by a comma or *and* has been added when appropriate. The ampersand (&) has been replaced, usually, by *and* or by a comma in a series or by a period after a complete thought. The ampersand has been deleted, without ellipses, when it refers to additional discussion not reported.

It is important that readers understand the inherent limitations of this Bible commentary as well as of any collection of Joseph Smith's teachings. The material collected here is only as accurate as the scribes who recorded the Prophet's words. The passages from sermons have unavoidably been filtered to some degree through the mind, the doctrinal understanding, and the vocabulary of those who kept the records. It is likely that the reliability of the records was not always consistent; the scribes may have done their work with varying degrees of precision. Thus, although I am confident that the recorders preserved the Prophet's message with remarkable skill, I am sure they would join with me in expressing caution about the infallibility of individual words or phrases. Moreover, my selecting and editing, however cautiously done, also involve some interpretation. It has

---

[7]Including tense, person, number, and case.

been my constant effort to compile this book so as to be true to the Prophet Joseph Smith and his message.

The Prophet's statements in this volume are arranged in biblical order, that is, beginning with Genesis and ending with Revelation. Some of the passages can be read and understood without reference to the biblical texts, but most respond directly to verses of the Bible and cannot be understood fully unless the corresponding scriptural passage is read first.

I express my sincere appreciation to able assistants who have helped me prepare this book, to kind colleagues whose wisdom has improved it, and to the staff of Deseret Book Company for their fine work in its production. But I am especially thankful for and to the Prophet Joseph Smith for teaching us how to read and understand the Bible and for the noble individuals who recorded his words to bless the lives of later generations.

Abbreviations

KFD Donald Q. Cannon and Larry E. Dahl, eds., *The Prophet Joseph Smith's King Follett Discourse: A Six-Column Comparison of Original Notes and Amalgamations* (Provo, Utah: Religious Studies Center, Brigham Young University, 1983).

PJS Dean C. Jessee, ed., *The Papers of Joseph Smith, Vol. 1: Autobiographical and Historical Writings* (Salt Lake City: Deseret Book, 1989); *Vol. 2: Journal, 1832–1842* (Salt Lake City: Deseret Book, 1992); *Vol. 3: Journal, 1842–1844* (Salt Lake City: Deseret Book, 1995).

PWJS Dean C. Jessee, ed., *The Personal Writings of Joseph Smith* (Salt Lake City: Deseret Book, 1984).

WJS Andrew F. Ehat and Lyndon W. Cook, eds., *The Words of Joseph Smith: The Contemporary Accounts of the Nauvoo Discourses of the Prophet Joseph* (Orem, Utah: Grandin Book, 1991).

Genesis

Genesis 1:1

The world and earth are not synonymous terms. The world is the human family. This earth was organized or formed out of other planets which were broken up and remodeled and made into the one on which we live. The elements are eternal. . . . The word "created" should be "formed" or "organized."[1]

God did not make the earth out of nothing, for it is contrary to a rational mind and reason that a something could be brought from a nothing. Also, it is contrary to the principle and means by which God does work. For instance, when God formed man, he made him of something—the dust of the earth—and he always took a something to affect a something else. . . . The earth was made out of something, for it is impossible for a something to be made out of nothing. Fire, air, and water are eternal existent principles, which are the composition of which the earth has been composed. Also, earth has been organized out of portions of other globes that have been disorganized, in testimony that this earth was not the first of God's work.[2]

I shall go to the first Hebrew word in the Bible—the first sentence. "In the beginning," *berō'shît.*[3] [*Be-*]: "in," "by," "through," and everything else; *rō'sh:* the "head." When the inspired man wrote it, he did not put the first part to it. A man, a Jew without any authority, thought it too bad to begin to talk about the head of any man. "The head one of the Gods brought forth the Gods" is the true meaning of the word. . . . Thus the head God brought

---

[1]Discourse of 5 January 1841, recorded by William Clayton; *WJS,* 60.

[2]Discourse of 5 January 1841, recorded by William P. McIntire; *WJS,* 61.

[3]The first word of the Hebrew Bible is *berē'shît.* The Prophet's revised pronunciation of it harmonizes with the interpretation and origin of the word that he taught in this discourse.

1

forth the Gods in the head council. . . . The head God called together the Gods and sat in [the] Grand Council. . . .

The learned men who are preaching salvation say that God created the heavens and the earth out of nothing, and the reason is that they are unlearned. I know more than all the world put together, and if the Holy Ghost in me comprehends more than all the world, I will associate with it. What does *bārā'* mean? It means to organize, same as you would organize a ship. God himself had materials to organize the world out of—chaos, which is element and in which dwells all the glory, that nothing can destroy. They never can have an ending; they coexist eternally.[4]

[I will] make a comment on the first sentence of the history of creation. *Berō'shît:* [I] want to analyze the word. *Be-:* "in," "by," "through," and everything else; *rō'sh:* the "head"; *-ît.* Where does it come from? When the inspired man wrote, he did not put the *be-* there. But a Jew put it there. It read in the first, "The head one of the Gods brought forth the Gods." [That] is the true meaning. . . . The grand councilors sat in yonder heavens and contemplated the creation of the worlds that were created at that time. . . .

Learned doctors[5] tell us God created the heavens and earth out of nothing. They account it blasphemy to contradict the idea. They will call you a fool. You ask them why. They say, "Doesn't the Bible say he created the world?" And they infer that it must be out of nothing. The word create came from the word *bārā'.* [It] doesn't mean so; it means to organize, same as [a] man would use to build a ship. Hence we infer that God had materials to organize from—chaos, chaotic matter. Element had an existence from the time [God] had. The pure principles of

---

[4]Discourse of 7 April 1844, recorded by Thomas Bullock; *KFD,* 37, 39, 45, 47.

[5]In this discourse the Prophet defined the "doctors" and "lawyers" against whom he preached: "When I say 'doctor' and 'lawyer,' I mean the doctors and lawyers of the scriptures." Report of William Clayton; *KFD,* 38.

element are principles that never can be destroyed; they may be organized and reorganized, but not destroyed.[6]

Create, *bārā'* in Hebrew, means [to] organize from chaos, or element.[7]

The head one of the Gods brought forth the Gods. . . . The head one called the Gods together in [the] Grand Council to bring forth the world. . . . In the beginning, the head of the Gods called a council of the Gods and concocted a scheme to create this world. . . .

[The] doctors say, [God] created the earth out of nothing. *Bārā'*, "create"; it meant to organize. God had materials to organize the world. Element—nothing can destroy [it]. [It has] no beginning, no end.[8]

The head one of the Gods brought forth the Gods. I will transpose it in the English language. I want you to know and learn that the Holy Ghost knows something. The Grand Council sat at the head and contemplated the creation of the world. . . . The Gods came together and concocted the plan of making the world and the inhabitants. . . .

The learned doctor says the Lord made the world out of nothing. You tell them that God made the world out of something, and they think you are a fool. But I am learned and know more than the whole world—the Holy Ghost does, anyhow, and I will associate myself with it. *Bārā':* to organize the world out of

---

[6]Discourse of 7 April 1844, recorded by William Clayton; *KFD,* 36, 38, 44, 46.

[7]Discourse of 7 April 1844, recorded by Samuel W. Richards; *WJS,* 361.

[8]Discourse of 7 April 1844, recorded by Willard Richards; *KFD,* 36, 38, 42, 46.

chaotic matter. Element—they are principles that cannot be dissolved; they may be reorganized.[9]

The first word shows a plurality of Gods. . . . *Berō'shît,* etc.: "In the beginning." *Rō'shît:* "the head." . . . *'Elōhîm: 'Elôah,* "God" in singular; *-îm* renders "Gods." . . . The head God organized the heavens and the earth. I defy all the learning in the world to refute me. In the beginning, the heads of the Gods organized the heaven and the earth.[10]

In the beginning, the head Gods organized the earth and the heavens.[11]

Genesis 1:2

In the translation "without form and void," it should read "empty and desolate."[12]

Genesis 1:11–12

It is a decree of the Lord that every tree, fruit, or herb bearing seed should bring forth after its kind and cannot come forth after any other law or principle.[13]

Genesis 1:14–18

God set the sun, the moon, and the stars in the heavens and gave them their laws, conditions, and bounds which they cannot pass except by his command. They all move in perfect harmony

---

[9]Discourse of 7 April 1844, recorded by Wilford Woodruff; *KFD,* 36, 38, 42, 44, 46.

[10]Discourse of 16 June 1844, recorded by Thomas Bullock; *WJS,* 379.

[11]Discourse of 16 June 1844, recorded by William P. McIntire; *WJS,* 383.

[12]Discourse of 5 January 1841, recorded by William Clayton; *WJS,* 60.

[13]Discourse of 20 March 1842, recorded by Wilford Woodruff; *WJS,* 107.

in their sphere and order and are as wonders, lights, and signs unto us.[14]

Genesis 1:26–28a

The priesthood was first given to Adam; he obtained the first presidency and held the keys of it from generation to generation. He obtained it in the creation before the world was formed. He had dominion given him over every living creature. He is Michael, the Archangel spoken of in the scriptures. Then to Noah, who is Gabriel. . . . These men held keys, first on earth, and then in heaven.

The priesthood is an everlasting principle and existed with God from eternity and will to eternity, without beginning of days or end of years. The keys have to be brought from heaven whenever the gospel is sent. When they are revealed from heaven, it is by Adam's authority. . . . The Father called all spirits before him at the creation of man and organized them. He (Adam) is the head; [he] was told to multiply. The keys were given to him and by him to others, and he will have to give an account of his stewardship, and they to him.[15]

Christ is the great High Priest, Adam next.[16]

The Melchizedek Priesthood . . . is the channel through which the Almighty commenced revealing his glory at the beginning of the creation of this earth, through which he has continued to reveal himself to the children of men to the present time, and through which he will make known his purposes to the end of time—commencing with Adam, who was the first man, who is

---

[14]Discourse of 20 March 1842, recorded by Wilford Woodruff; *WJS,* 107.

[15]Discourse of summer of 1839, recorded in Willard Richards's "Pocket Companion"; *WJS,* 8–9.

[16]Discourse of summer of 1839, recorded in Willard Richards's "Pocket Companion"; *WJS,* 9.

spoken of in Daniel as being the "Ancient of Days" [Dan. 7:9–14], or in other words the first and oldest of all, the great grand progenitor of whom it is said in another place, he is Michael [D&C 107:54], because he was the first and father of all, not only by progeny, but he was the first to hold the spiritual blessings, to whom was made known the plan of ordinances for the salvation of his posterity unto the end, to whom Christ was first revealed, and through whom Christ has been revealed from heaven and will continue to be revealed from henceforth. Adam holds the keys of the Dispensation of the Fulness of Times, that is, the dispensation of all the times [that] have been and will be revealed through him from the beginning to Christ and from Christ to the end of all the dispensations that have [been and] are to be revealed.[17]

There has been a chain of authority and power from Adam down to the present time.[18]

See also under Daniel 7:9–14.

Genesis 1:26–28b

That which is without body or parts is nothing. There is no other God in heaven but that God who has flesh and bones. "As the Father hath life in himself, even so hath he given the Son to have life in himself" [John 5:26]. God the Father took life unto himself precisely as Jesus did. The first step in the salvation of men is the laws of eternal and self-existent principles. Spirits are eternal. At the first organization in heaven, we were all present and saw the Savior chosen and appointed and the plan of salvation made. And we sanctioned it. We came to this earth that we

---

[17]Discourse of 5 October 1840, recorded by Robert B. Thompson; *WJS,* 38–39.

[18]Discourse of 3 October 1841, reported in *Times and Seasons,* 15 October 1841, 577.

might have a body and present it pure before God in the Celestial kingdom.[19]

After God had created the heavens and the earth, he came down and on the sixth day said, "Let us make man in our own image." In whose image? In the image of Gods created they them, male and female: innocent, harmless, and spotless, bearing the same character and the same image as the Gods. And when man fell he did not lose his image but his character, still retaining the image of his maker, Christ, who is the image of man [and] is also the express image of his Father's person. . . . And through the atonement of Christ and the resurrection and obedience in the gospel, we shall again be conformed to the image of his Son Jesus Christ. Then we shall have attained to the image, glory, and character of God.[20]

What was the design of the Almighty in making man? It was to exalt him to be as God.[21]

God himself, who sits enthroned in yonder heavens, is a man like unto one of yourselves. [He] who holds this world in its orbit and upholds all things by his power—if you were to see him today you would see him a man. For Adam was a man in fashion and image like unto him. Adam walked, talked, and communed with him as one man talks and communes with another.[22]

God, that sits enthroned, is a man like one of yourselves. That is the great secret. If the veil were rent today and the great God, who holds this world in its sphere or its orbit, and the planets— if you were to see him today you would see him in all the person,

---

[19]Discourse of 5 January 1841, recorded by William Clayton; *WJS,* 60.

[20]Discourse of 9 July 1843, recorded by James Burgess; *WJS,* 231.

[21]Discourse of 27 August 1843, recorded by James Burgess; *WJS,* 247.

[22]Discourse of 7 April 1844, recorded by Thomas Bullock; *KFD,* 27.

image, [and] very form of man. For Adam was created in the very fashion of God. Adam received instruction, walked, [and] talked [with God] as one man with another.[23]

[God] is a man like one of yourselves. Should you see him today, you would see a man in fashion and in form. Adam was formed in his likeness.[24]

God, who sits in yonder heavens, is a man like yourselves. That God that holds the worlds, if you were to see him today, you would see him like a man in form like yourselves. Adam was made in his image and talked with him and walked with him.[25]

The head one of the Gods said, "Let us make man in our image."[26]

Genesis 2:7

In tracing the thing to the foundation and looking at it philo-sophically, we shall find a very material difference between the body and the spirit. The body is supposed to be organized matter, and the spirit by many is thought to be immaterial, without substance. With this latter statement we should beg leave to differ and state that spirit is a substance, that it is material, but that it is more pure, elastic, and refined matter than the body—that it existed before the body, can exist in the body, and will exist separate from the body, when the body will be moldering in the dust, and will in the resurrection be again united with it. Without attempting to describe this mysterious connection and the laws that govern the body and spirit of man, their relationship to each

---

[23]Discourse of 7 April 1844, recorded by William Clayton; *KFD,* 26.

[24]Discourse of 7 April 1844, recorded by Willard Richards; *KFD,* 26.

[25]Discourse of 7 April 1844, recorded by Wilford Woodruff; *KFD,* 26.

[26]Discourse of 16 June 1844, recorded by Thomas Bullock; *WJS,* 379.

other, and the design of God in relation to the human body and spirit, I would just remark that the spirits of men are eternal, that they are governed by the same priesthood that Abraham, Melchizedek, and the apostles were, that they are organized according to that priesthood which is everlasting—"without beginning of days or end of years" [Heb. 7:3]—that they all move in their respective spheres and are governed by the law of God, that when they appear upon the earth they are in a probationary state and are preparing, if righteous, for a future and a greater glory.[27]

When God breathed into man's nostrils he became a living soul. Before that he did not live, and when that was taken away his body died.[28]

The 7th verse of chapter 2 of Genesis ought to read, "God breathed into Adam his spirit, or breath of life." . . . There is no such thing as immaterial matter. All spirit is matter but is more fine or pure and can only be discerned by purer eyes. We cannot see it, but when our bodies are purified we shall see that it is all matter.[29]

The soul, the immortal spirit of man, [the learned] says [God] created [it] in the beginning. The very idea lessens man in my idea. I don't believe the doctrine. Hear it, all ye ends of the world, for God has told me so. I am going to tell of things more noble. We say that God himself is a self-existing God. Who told you so? How did it get into your head? Who told you that man did not exist in like manner? How does it read in the Hebrew?— that God made man and put into it Adam's spirit, and so [he] became a living spirit. The mind of man—the mind of man is as

---

[27]*Times and Seasons,* 1 April 1842, 745.

[28]*Times and Seasons,* 1 April 1842, 746.

[29]Discourse of 17 May 1843, recorded by William Clayton; *WJS,* 203; see D&C 131:7–8.

immortal as God himself. Hence, while I talk to these mourners, they are only separated from their bodies for a short period. Their spirits coexisted with God and now converse [with] one another, same as we do. Does not this give you satisfaction? I want to reason more on the spirit of man, for I am dwelling on the body of man, on the subject of the dead. I take my ring from my finger and liken it unto the mind of man, the immortal spirit, because it has no beginning. Suppose you cut it in two. But as the Lord lives, there would be an end. All the fools and wise men from the beginning of creation who say that man had [a] beginning—they must have an end, and then the doctrine of annihilation would be true. But if I am right, I might with boldness proclaim from the housetop that God never had power to create the spirit of man at all. God himself could not create himself. Intelligence is self-existent. It is a spirit from age to end, and there is no creation about it.[30]

The soul, the mind of man, they say God created it in the beginning. The idea lessens man, in my estimation. [I] don't believe the doctrine [and] know better; God told me so. . . . We say that God was self-existent. Who told you so? It's correct enough, but how did it get into your heads? Who told you that man did not exist upon the same principle? [It] doesn't say so in the old Hebrew. God made man out of the earth and put into him his spirit, and then it became a living body. The mind of man, the intelligent part, is coequal[31] with God himself. I know that my testimony is true. Hence, when I talk to these mourners, what have they lost? They are only separated from their bodies for a short season. But their spirits existed coequal with God, and they now exist in a place where they converse together as much as we

---

[30]Discourse of 7 April 1844, recorded by Thomas Bullock; *KFD*, 49, 51.

[31]It appears from the context that the word *coequal* here means "coeval," or "coeternal."

do on the earth. Is it logic to say that a spirit is immortal and yet has a beginning? Because if a spirit has a beginning, it will have an end. [That is] good logic. All the fools, learned, and wise men that come and tell that man has a beginning prove that he must have an end. And if that doctrine is true, then the doctrine of annihilation is true. But if I am right, then I might be bold to say that God never did have power to create the spirit of man at all. He could not create himself. Intelligence exists upon a self-existing principle. [It] is a spirit from age to age, and [there is] no creation about it.[32]

The soul, the mind of man, where did it come from? The learned says God made it in the beginning, but it is not so. I know better; God has told me so. If you don't believe it, it won't make the truth without effect. God was a self-existing being; man exists upon the same principle. God made a tabernacle and put a spirit in it, and it became a human soul. Man existed in spirit and mind coequal with God himself. You who mourn the loss of friends are only separated for a moment; the spirit is separated for a little time. They are now conversant with each other as we are on the earth. I am dwelling on the immutability of the spirit of man. Is it logic to say the spirit of man had a beginning and yet had no end? It does not have a beginning or end. My ring is like the existence of man; it has no beginning or end. If cut in two, there would be a beginning and end. So with man; if it had a beginning it will have an end. If I am right, I might say God never had power to create the spirit of man. God himself could not create himself. Intelligence is eternal, and it is self-existing.[33]

See also under Genesis 1:26–28b.

---

[32]Discourse of 7 April 1844, recorded by William Clayton; *KFD*, 48, 50.

[33]Discourse of 7 April 1844, recorded by Wilford Woodruff; *KFD*, 48, 50.

Genesis 2:15–17

It may be supposed, and we think with a degree of propriety, that man had given to him in the beginning, from the hand of his Maker, every necessary law and instruction for his peace, happiness, and future comfort. And if not, living as he did in the immediate presence and walking under the inspection of heaven, if he needed more he could yet ask it, and that wise hand which had formed him of the dust was sufficient, not only sufficient, but knowing all things, knew whether man needed more or not. And if he did, it would be bestowed. To suppose that the Maker of the universe never gave to man any law after he had formed him would, in our opinion, be offering an insult to his glorious character and be comparing him beneath even an earthly parent. For where, we ask, is the kind, humane father to be found who would, for any consideration whatever, suffer his children to grow up to manhood without giving them instruction, and instruction too which would be wisely calculated to benefit them even in ripened years? . . . Should the great author of our being, after he had made all things and even man and pronounced them all "good," leave man without a law, we might well suppose that here was a contradiction in terms indeed. For he had pronounced all things which he had made "good," and yet there was no good in man. Consequently, he was not worthy to receive a law whereby his conduct might be governed, but must be left without any principles or directions from the hand of his Maker to guide him in the least particular.[34]

Genesis 2:17

At the time the Lord said this to Adam, there was no mode of counting time by man, as man now counts time.[35]

See also under Genesis 3:6.

---

[34]*Evening and Morning Star,* March 1834, 143.

[35]Discourse of 9 March 1841, recorded by William P. McIntire; *WJS,* 64–65.

Genesis 2:21–24

Marriage is an institution of heaven, instituted in the garden of Eden; it is necessary that it should be solemnized by the authority of the everlasting priesthood.[36]

Marriage [is] an institution of heaven, first solemnized in the garden of Eden by God himself, by the authority of everlasting priesthood.[37]

Moses 4:1–6

When [Satan] fell, he sought for things which were unlawful. Hence he was cast down, and it is said he drew away many with him.[38]

Jesus contended that there would be certain souls that would be condemned, and the Devil said he could save them all. As the Grand Council gave in for Jesus Christ, so the Devil fell and all who put up their heads for him.[39]

The contention in heaven was [that] Jesus said there were certain men [who] would not be saved. The Devil said he could save them. He rebelled against God and was thrust down.[40]

[The] Devil said he could save them all. [The] lot fell on Jesus.[41]

---

[36]Journal, 24 November 1835; *PJS,* 2:89.

[37]1834–36 History, 24 November 1835; *PJS,* 1:146.

[38]Discourse of 14 May 1843, recorded by Wilford Woodruff; *WJS,* 201.

[39]Discourse of 7 April 1844, recorded by Thomas Bullock; *KFD,* 64.

[40]Discourse of 7 April 1844, recorded by William Clayton; *KFD,* 64.

[41]Discourse of 7 April 1844, recorded by Willard Richards; *KFD,* 64.

The Devil said, "I am a Savior and can save all." [He] rose up in rebellion against God and was cast down.[42]

The Devil, Lucifer, also organized his kingdom in opposition to overthrow God's kingdom, and he became the son of perdition.[43]

Genesis 3:6

Adam did not commit sin in eating the fruits, for God had decreed that he should eat and fall. But in compliance with the decree, he should die. Only [that] he should die was the saying of the Lord; therefore the Lord appointed us to fall and also redeemed us.[44]

Genesis 3:9–10

God called Adam by his own voice.[45]

Moses 5:4–8

Perhaps our friends will say that the gospel and its ordinances were not known till the days of John the son of Zacharias in the days of Herod the king of Judea. But we will here look at this point. For our own part, we cannot believe that the ancients in all ages were so ignorant of the system of heaven as many suppose, since all that were ever saved were saved through the power of this great plan of redemption, as much so before the coming of Christ as since. If not, God has had different plans in operation (if we may so express it) to bring men back to dwell

---

[42]Discourse of 7 April 1844, recorded by Wilford Woodruff; *KFD*, 64.

[43]Discourse of 12 May 1844, recorded by George Laub; *WJS*, 370.

[44]Discourse of 9 February 1841, recorded by William P. McIntire; *WJS*, 63.

[45]Discourse of 5 October 1840, recorded by Robert B. Thompson; *WJS*, 40.

with himself. And this we cannot believe, since there has been no change in the constitution of man since he fell. And the ordinance or institution of offering blood in sacrifice was only designed to be performed till Christ was offered up and shed his blood, that man might look forward with faith to that time. . . . We conclude that whenever the Lord revealed himself to men in ancient days and commanded them to offer sacrifice to him, that it was done that they might look forward in faith to the time of his coming and rely upon the power of that Atonement for a remission of their sins. And this they have done, thousands who have gone before us, whose garments are spotless and who are, like Job, waiting with an assurance like his that they will see him in the latter day upon the earth, even in their flesh [Job 19:25–26].

We may conclude that though there were different dispensations, yet all things which God communicated to his people were calculated to draw their minds to the great object, and to teach them to rely upon him alone as the author of their salvation, as contained in his law.[46]

God will not acknowledge that which he has not called, ordained, and chosen. . . . Adam received commandments and instruction from God. This was the order from the beginning. That he received revelations, commandments, and ordinances at the beginning is beyond the power of controversy, else how did they begin to offer sacrifices to God in an acceptable manner? And if they offered sacrifices, they must be authorized by ordination.[47]

Moses 5:12–15

It is reasonable to suppose that man departed from the first

---

[46]*Evening and Morning Star,* March 1834, 143.

[47]Discourse of 5 October 1840, recorded by Robert B. Thompson; *WJS,* 40.

teachings or instructions which he received from heaven in the first age and refused by his disobedience to be governed by them. Consequently, he formed such laws as best suited his own mind or, as he supposed, were best adapted to his situation. . . . But notwithstanding this transgression, by which man had cut himself off from an immediate intercourse with his Maker without a Mediator, it appears that the great and glorious plan of his redemption was previously mediated, the sacrifice prepared, [and] the Atonement wrought out in the mind and purpose of God, even in the person of the Son, through whom man was now to look for acceptance and through whose merits he was now taught that he alone could find redemption, since the word had been pronounced, "Unto dust thou shalt return" [Gen. 3:19].

But that man was not sufficient of himself to erect a system or plan with power sufficient to free him from a destruction which awaited him is evident from the fact that God, as before remarked, prepared a sacrifice in the gift of his own Son, which should be sent in due time in his own wisdom, to prepare a way or open a door through which man might enter into his presence, from whence he had been cast for disobedience.[48]

Genesis 4:3–12

By faith in this Atonement, or plan of redemption, Abel offered to God a sacrifice that was accepted, which was the firstlings of the flock. Cain offered of the fruit of the ground and was not accepted, because he could not do it in faith. He could have no faith, or could not exercise faith, contrary to the plan of heaven. It must be the shedding of the blood of the Only Begotten to atone for man, for this was the plan of redemption, and without the shedding of blood was no remission. And as the sacrifice was instituted for a type by which man was to discern the great sacrifice which God had prepared, to offer a sacrifice

---

[48]*Evening and Morning Star,* March 1834, 143.

contrary to that, no faith could be exercised, because redemption was not purchased in that way, nor the power of atonement instituted after that order. Consequently, Cain could have no faith, and "whatsoever is not of faith is sin" [Rom. 14:23]. But Abel offered an acceptable sacrifice by which he obtained witness that he was righteous, God himself testifying of his gifts [Heb. 11:4]. Certainly, the shedding of the blood of a beast could be beneficial to no man, except it was done in imitation, or as a type or explanation, of what was to be offered through the gift of God himself, and this performance done with an eye looking forward in faith on the power of that great sacrifice for a remission of sins.

But however various may have been, and may be at the present time, the opinions of men respecting the conduct of Abel and the knowledge which he had on the subject of atonement, it is evident in our minds that he was instructed more fully into the plan than what the Bible speaks. For how could he offer a sacrifice in faith, looking to God for a remission of his sins in the power of the great Atonement, without having been previously instructed in that plan? And further, if he was accepted of God, what were the ordinances performed further than the offering of the firstlings of the flock? It is said by Paul in his letter to his Hebrew brethren that Abel obtained witness that he was righteous, God testifying of his gifts. To whom did God testify of the gifts of Abel. Was it to Paul? We have very little on this important subject in the forepart of the Bible. But it is said that Abel himself obtained witness that he was righteous. Then certainly God spoke to him. Indeed, it is said that God talked with him. And if he did, would he not, seeing he was righteous, deliver to him the whole plan of the gospel? And is not the gospel the news of redemption? How could Abel offer a sacrifice and look forward with faith on the Son of God for a remission of his sins and not understand the gospel? The mere shedding [of] the blood of beasts or offering anything else in sacrifice could not procure a remission of sins, except it were performed in faith of something to come. If it could, Cain's offering must have been as good as

Abel's. And if Abel was taught of the coming of the Son of God, was he not taught of his ordinances? We all admit that the gospel has ordinances, and if so, had it not always ordinances, and were not its ordinances always the same?[49]

All knowledge comes from God, yet when it has been revealed, all men have not believed it as revelation at the time. Hence, when Abel's offering was accepted of the Lord, that knowledge must have been communicated by revelation. And that revelation, though it gave Abel power with God, still Cain was offended, disbelieved, and committed murder. Cain knew the Lord and believed in his father Adam's scripture, or revelation. But one revelation was enough; he could not bear new ones and fell.[50]

Genesis 4:4

See under Hebrews 11:4.

Genesis 4:5

The power, glory, and blessings of the priesthood could not continue with [all] those who received ordination, [but] only as their righteousness continued. For Cain also being authorized to offer sacrifice but not offering it in righteousness, therefore he was cursed. It signifies, then, that the ordinances must be kept in the very way God has appointed; otherwise their priesthood will prove a cursing instead of a blessing. If Cain had fulfilled the law of righteousness as did Enoch, he could have walked with God all the days of his life and never failed of a blessing.[51]

---

[49]*Evening and Morning Star,* March 1834, 143.

[50]*Times and Seasons,* 15 August 1842, 889.

[51]Discourse of 5 October 1840, recorded by Robert B. Thompson; *WJS,* 40–41.

Genesis 5:5; D&C 107:53–57

I saw Adam in the valley of Adam-ondi-Ahman. He called together his children and blessed them with a patriarchal blessing. The Lord appeared in their midst. And Adam blessed them all and foretold what should befall them to the latest generation.[52]

Moses 7:62

God clearly manifested to Enoch the redemption which he prepared by offering the Messiah as a Lamb slain from before the foundation of the world, [and] by virtue of the same the glorious resurrection of the Savior and the resurrection of all the human family, even a resurrection of their corporeal bodies, and also righteousness and truth to sweep the earth as with a flood. Now I ask how righteousness and truth are going to sweep the earth as with a flood. I will answer: Men and angels are to be co-workers in bringing to pass this great work, and a Zion is to be prepared—even a new Jerusalem—for the elect that are to be gathered from the four quarters of the earth, and to be established an holy city. For the tabernacle of the Lord shall be with them.[53]

Genesis 5:24; Moses 7:69

Now this Enoch, God reserved unto himself that he should not die at that time and appointed unto him a ministry unto terrestrial bodies, of whom there has been but little revealed. He is reserved also unto the presidency of a dispensation. . . . He is a ministering angel, to minister to those who shall be heirs of salvation, and [he] appeared unto Jude as Abel did unto Paul. . . .

Now the doctrine of translation is a power which belongs to this priesthood. There are many things which belong to the powers of the priesthood and the keys thereof that have been kept hid

---

[52]Discourse of summer of 1839, recorded in Willard Richards's "Pocket Companion"; *WJS*, 9.

[53]*Messenger and Advocate*, November 1835, 209.

from before the foundation of the world. They are hid from the wise and prudent to be revealed in the last times. Many may have supposed that the doctrine of translation was a doctrine whereby men were taken immediately into the presence of God and into an eternal fulness. But this is a mistaken idea. Their place of habitation is that of the terrestrial order and a place prepared for such characters he held in reserve to be ministering angels unto many planets, and who as yet have not entered into so great a fulness as those who are resurrected from the dead.[54]

He selected Enoch, whom he directed, and gave his law unto [him] and to the people who were with him. And when the world in general would not obey the commands of God, after walking with God he translated Enoch and his church, and the priesthood or government of heaven was taken away.[55]

If Enoch was righteous enough to come into the presence of God and walk with him, he must have become so by keeping his commandments—and so of every righteous person.[56]

Genesis 5:28–31

The priesthood continued from Lamech to Noah.[57]

Genesis 6:6

As it reads, "it repented the Lord that he had made man" ([but] also, "God is not a man . . . that he should repent" [Num. 23:19]), which I do not believe. But, "it repented Noah that God

---

[54]Discourse of 5 October 1840, recorded by Robert B. Thompson; *WJS*, 41.

[55]*Times and Seasons*, 15 July 1842, 857.

[56]*Times and Seasons*, 1 September 1842, 905.

[57]Discourse of 5 October 1840, recorded by Robert B. Thompson; *WJS*, 42.

made man." This I believe, and then the other quotation stands fair.[58]

Genesis 6:9–13

The priesthood was first given to Adam. . . . Then to Noah, who is Gabriel; he stands next in authority to Adam in the priesthood. He was called of God to this office and was the father of all living in his day, and to him was given the dominion.[59]

The keys of this priesthood consisted in obtaining the voice of Jehovah, that he talked with [Noah] in a familiar and friendly manner, that he continued to him the keys, the covenants, the power, and the glory with which he blessed Adam at the beginning.[60]

Noah was a perfect man, and his knowledge or revelation of what was to take place upon the earth gave him power to prepare and save himself and family from the destruction of the flood. This knowledge, or revelation, was not believed by the inhabitants of the earth. . . . They could not endure the new revelation: "The old we believe because our fathers did, but away with new revelations!"—and the flood swept them away.[61]

Now taking it for granted that the scriptures say what they mean and mean what they say, we have sufficient grounds to go on and prove from the Bible that the gospel has always been the same, the ordinances to fulfil its requirements the same, the officers to officiate the same, and the signs and fruits resulting from

---

[58]Discourse of 15 October 1843, recorded by Willard Richards; *WJS*, 256.

[59]Discourse of summer of 1839, recorded in Willard Richards's "Pocket Companion"; *WJS*, 8.

[60]Discourse of 5 October 1840, recorded by Robert B. Thompson; *WJS*, 42.

[61]*Times and Seasons*, 15 August 1842, 889–90.

the promises the same. Therefore, as Noah was a preacher of righteousness, he must have been baptized and ordained to the priesthood by the laying on of the hands, and so forth.[62]

Genesis 8:21–22

See under Matthew 24:36.

Genesis 9:9–17

See under Matthew 24:36.

Genesis 12:1–5

The word spoken to Noah was not sufficient for Abraham, or it was not required of Abraham to leave the land of his nativity and seek an inheritance in a strange country upon the word spoken to Noah. But for himself he obtained promises at the hand of the Lord and walked in [such] perfection that he was called the friend of God.[63]

Abraham was guided in all his family affairs by the Lord, was told where to go and when to stop, was conversed with by angels and by the Lord, and prospered exceedingly in all that he put his hand unto. It was because he and his family obeyed the counsel of the Lord.[64]

Abraham [came] with the knowledge, or revelation, and what is the result? Why, he becomes a pilgrim in a strange land; nobody believed in his religion because he had new revelations.[65]

---

[62]*Times and Seasons,* 1 September 1842, 904.

[63]Letter to Silas Smith, from Kirtland, Ohio, 26 September 1833; *PWJS,* 298.

[64]*Times and Seasons,* 15 July 1842, 857.

[65]*Times and Seasons,* 15 August 1842, 890.

Genesis 14:18–20

See under Hebrews 7:1–11.

Genesis 14:18

It is understood by many . . . that Melchizedek was king of some country or nation on the earth. But it was not so. In the original it reads "king of Shalom," which signifies king of peace or righteousness, and not of any country or nation.[66]

The word "Salem" is a wrong translation. It should be "Shalom," signifying peace.[67]

"Salem" is designed for a Hebrew term. It should be "Shalom," which signifies righteousness and peace. As it is, it is nothing—neither Hebrew, Greek, Latin, French, or any other.[68]

Genesis 15:12, JST

See under Galatians 3:8.

Genesis 17:9–14

Circumcision was merely a *sign* of the priesthood, given to Abraham.[69]

Genesis 19:1–25

God sent angels to gather [Lot] and his family out of Sodom, while the wicked were destroyed by a devouring fire.[70]

---

[66]Discourse of 27 August 1843, recorded by James Burgess; *WJS,* 246.

[67]Discourse of 27 August 1843, recorded by William Clayton; *WJS,* 247.

[68]Discourse of 27 August 1843, recorded by Willard Richards; *WJS,* 244.

[69]*Times and Seasons,* 1 September 1842, 904.

[70]Letter to W. W. Phelps, from Hiram, Ohio, 31 July 1832; *PWJS,* 247.

Genesis 19:24–25

In consequence of rejecting the gospel of Jesus Christ and the prophets whom God has sent, the judgments of God have rested upon people, cities, and nations in various ages of the world, which was the case with the cities of Sodom and Gomorrah, who were destroyed for rejecting the prophets.[71]

Genesis 22:1–12

Men will set up stakes and say, "Thus far will we go and no farther." Did Abraham, when called upon to offer his son?[72]

Genesis 22:15–18

[Abraham obtained] power, even power of an endless life, . . . by the offering of his son Isaac, which was not the power of a prophet, nor apostle, nor patriarch only, but of [a] king and priest to God—to open the windows of heaven and pour out the peace and law of endless life to man.[73]

If a man would attain, he must sacrifice all to attain to the keys of the kingdom of an endless life.[74]

Genesis 26:3–5

Isaac, the promised seed, was not required to rest his hope upon the promises made to his father, Abraham, but was privileged with the assurance of his approbation in the sight of heaven by the direct voice of the Lord to him. If one man can live upon the revelations given to another, might not I, with propriety, ask why the necessity then of the Lord speaking to Isaac as he did,

---

[71]Discourse of 22 January 1843, recorded by Wilford Woodruff; *WJS,* 156.

[72]Discourse of 27 August 1843, recorded by James Burgess; *WJS,* 246.

[73]Discourse of 27 August 1843, recorded by Franklin D. Richards; *WJS,* 245.

[74]Discourse of 27 August 1843, recorded by Willard Richards; *WJS,* 244.

as is recorded in the 26th chapter of Genesis. For the Lord there repeats, or rather promises again, to perform the oath which he had previously sworn unto Abraham. And why this repetition to Isaac? Why was not the first promise as sure for Isaac as it was for Abraham? Was not Isaac Abraham's son, and could he not place implicit confidence in the word of his father as being a man of God?

Perhaps you may say that he was a very peculiar man and different from men in these last days, consequently the Lord favored him with blessings peculiar and different, as he was different from men in this age. I admit that he was a peculiar man and was not only peculiarly blessed but greatly blessed. But all the peculiarity that I can discover in the man, or all the difference between him and men in this age, is that he was more holy and more perfect before God and came to him with a purer heart and more faith than men in this day. . . .

Isaac obtained a renewal of the covenant made to Abraham by the direct voice of the Lord.[75]

Genesis 28:20–22

And now, O Father, as thou didst prosper our father Jacob and bless him with protection and prosperity wherever he went, from the time he made a like covenant before and with thee; and as thou didst, even the same night, open the heavens unto him and manifest great mercy and favor and give him promises—so wilt thou do by us his sons? And as his blessings prevailed above the blessings of his progenitors unto the utmost bounds of the everlasting hills, even so may our blessings prevail like his. And may thy servants be preserved from the power and influence of wicked and unrighteous men. May every weapon formed against us fall upon the head of him who shall form it. May we be

---

[75]Letter to Silas Smith, from Kirtland, Ohio, 26 September 1833; *PWJS,* 298–99, 300.

blessed with a name and a place among thy Saints here, and thy sanctified when they shall rest.[76]

Genesis 49

An evangelist is a patriarch, even the oldest man of the blood of Joseph or of the seed of Abraham. Wherever the Church of Christ is established in the earth, there should be a patriarch for the benefit of the posterity of the Saints, as it was with Jacob in giving his patriarchal blessing unto his sons.[77]

---

[76]Journal, 29 November 1834; *PJS* 2:35.

[77]Discourse of 27 June 1839, recorded in Willard Richards's "Pocket Companion"; *WJS,* 6.

Exodus

Exodus 1:6–11

When Egypt was under the superintendence of Joseph, it prospered, because he was taught of God. When they oppressed the Israelites, destruction came upon them.[1]

Exodus 4:10–12

Moses was a stuttering sort of a boy like me.[2]

Exodus 7:8–12

The Egyptians were not able to discover the difference between the miracles of Moses and those of the magicians until they came to be tested together. And if Moses had not appeared in their midst they would unquestionably have thought that the miracles of the magicians were performed through the mighty power of God, for they were great miracles that were performed by them. A supernatural agency was developed and great power manifested. . . . Moses could detect the magicians' power and show that he was God's servant.[3]

Exodus 9:16

Why did God say to Pharaoh, "For this cause have I raised thee up"? Because Pharaoh was a fit instrument—a wicked man—and had committed acts of cruelty of the most atrocious nature.[4]

---

[1]*Times and Seasons,* 15 July 1842, 857.

[2]Discourse of 16 June 1844, recorded by Thomas Bullock; *WJS,* 381.

[3]*Times and Seasons,* 1 April 1842, 743, 745.

[4]Discourse of 16 May 1841, recorded by William Clayton; *WJS,* 73.

Exodus 14:13–31

We [are] like the children of Israel with the Red Sea before them and the Egyptians ready to fall upon them to destroy them, and no arm could deliver but the arm of God. And this is the case with us; we must wait on God to be gracious and call on him without ceasing to make bare his arm for our defence. For naught but the arm of the Almighty can save us.[5]

Exodus 19:3–8

When the children of Israel were chosen with Moses at their head, they were to be a peculiar people among whom God should place his name. Their motto was "The Lord is our lawgiver, the Lord is our judge, the Lord is our king, and he shall reign over us" [Isa. 33:22]. While in this state they might truly say, "Happy is that people whose God is the Lord" [Ps. 144:15]. Their government was a theocracy; they had God to make their laws and men chosen by him to administer them. He was their God, and they were his people. Moses received the word of the Lord from God himself. He was the mouth of God to Aaron, and Aaron taught the people in both civil and ecclesiastical affairs. They were both one; there was no distinction. So will it be when the purposes of God shall be accomplished, when "the Lord shall be king over the whole earth" [Zech. 14:9] and Jerusalem his throne.[6]

Exodus 20:1–2

[At] Mount Sinai, . . . Jesus gave the law to Moses.[7]

---

[5]Letter to W. W. Phelps, John Whitmer, Edward Partridge, Isaac Morley, John Corrill, and Sidney Gilbert, from Kirtland, Ohio, 18 August 1833; *PWJS*, 285.

[6]*Times and Seasons*, 15 July 1842, 857.

[7]Discourse of 23 July 1843, recorded by James Burgess; *WJS*, 235.

Moses, the man who wrote of Christ, . . . brought forth the law by commandment, as a school master to bring men to Christ.[8]

Exodus 20:13–17

These sentiments we most cordially embrace and consider them binding on us, because they are adapted to our circumstances.[9]

Exodus 20:18–19

When God offers a blessing or knowledge to a man and he refuses to receive it, he will be damned. [Such is] the case of the Israelites praying that God would speak to Moses and not to them, in consequence of which he cursed them with a carnal law.[10]

Exodus 30:30

See under Exodus 40:13–15.

Exodus 32:1–20

Men are as liable in this generation to turn aside from the holy commandments as were the children of Israel when Aaron bought the golden calf at the expense of all the jewelry and riches of the children of Israel, while Moses tarried yet forty days in the mount that he might receive the law of the everlasting gospel upon tables of stone, written by the finger of God, while they, the children of Israel, were delivered over and bowed down and worshiped the dumb idol and said, "These be our gods that brought

---

[8]*Times and Seasons,* 1 September 1842, 905.

[9]Letter to Isaac Galland, from Liberty Jail, Missouri, 22 March 1839; *Times and Seasons,* February 1840, 54.

[10]Discourse of 27 August 1843, recorded by William Clayton; *WJS,* 247.

us up out of the land of Egypt." And Moses, being angry, destroyed the tables of stone and the golden calf and made the children of Israel drink the substance of their god, which they said brought them up out of the land of Egypt.[11]

Exodus 32:19

See under Malachi 4:4.

Exodus 33:20, JST

See under Exodus 34:1–2, JST.

Exodus 34:1–2, JST

Moses sought to bring the children of Israel into the presence of God, through the power of the priesthood, but he could not.[12]

All priesthood is Melchizedek, but there are different portions or degrees of it. That portion which brought Moses to speak with God face to face was taken away, but that which brought the ministry of angels remained. All the prophets had the Melchizedek priesthood and were ordained by God himself.[13]

The law was given under Aaron for the purpose of pouring out judgments and destructions.[14]

Exodus 40:13–15

There was a priesthood conferred upon the sons of Levi throughout the generations of the Jews. They were born heirs to

---

[11]Letter to Edward Partridge, W. W. Phelps, and others, from Kirtland, Ohio, 30 March 1834; *PWJS,* 316–17.

[12]Discourse of summer of 1839, recorded in Willard Richards's "Pocket Companion"; *WJS,* 9.

[13]Discourse of 5 January 1841, recorded by William Clayton; *WJS,* 59.

[14]Discourse of 27 August 1843, recorded by Willard Richards; *WJS,* 244.

that priesthood by lineage or descent and held the keys of the first principles of the gospel.[15]

The priesthood was given to Aaron and his posterity throughout all generations. We can trace the lineage down to Zacharias, he being the only lawful administrator in his day.[16]

[It was] forever hereditary, fixed on the head of Aaron down to Zacharias, the father of John.[17]

---

[15]Discourse of 21 March 1841, recorded by William P. McIntire; *WJS*, 67.

[16]Discourse of 23 July 1843, recorded by James Burgess; *WJS*, 235.

[17]Discourse of 23 July 1843, recorded by Willard Richards; *WJS*, 234.

Leviticus

Leviticus 2:2–3

It is a very prevalent opinion that the sacrifices which were offered were entirely consumed. This was not the case. If you read Leviticus 2:2–3 you will observe that the priests took a part as a memorial and offered it up before the Lord, while the remainder was kept for the maintenance of the priests. So the offerings and sacrifices are not all consumed upon the altar, but the blood is sprinkled, and the fat and certain other portions are consumed.[1]

---

[1]Discourse of 5 October 1840, recorded by Robert Thompson; *WJS*, 43.

Deuteronomy

Deuteronomy 30:4

Mark carefully what the prophet says: "If any are driven out unto the utmost parts of heaven," which must mean the breadths of the earth. Now this promise is good to any, if there should be such, that are driven out, even in the last days. Therefore, the children of the fathers have claim unto this day.[1]

---

[1]*Messenger and Advocate,* November 1835, 210.

1 Samuel

1 Samuel 15:22

We have been chastened by the hand of God heretofore for not obeying his commands. . . . We have treated lightly his commands and departed from his ordinances. And the Lord has chastened us sore, and we have felt his arm and kissed the rod. Let us be wise in time to come and ever remember that "to obey is better than sacrifice, and to hearken than the fat of rams."[1]

---

[1]*Times and Seasons,* 15 July 1842, 857.

2 Samuel

2 Samuel 6:2–7

Men should not attempt to steady the ark of God.[1]

Many of the elders have come under great condemnation in endeavoring to steady the ark of God, in a place where they have not been sent.[2]

Man cannot steady the ark. My arm cannot do it; God must steady it.[3]

2 Samuel 12:7–13

A murderer, for instance, one that sheds innocent blood, cannot have forgiveness. David sought repentance at the hand of God, carefully with tears, but he could only get it through Hell. He got a promise that his soul should not be left in Hell. Although David was a king, he never did obtain the spirit and power of Elijah and the fulness of the priesthood. And the priesthood that he received and the throne and kingdom of David is to be taken from him and given to another by the name of David in the last days, raised up out of his lineage.[4]

See also under Acts 2:29, 34.

---

[1]Letter to Edward Partridge, W. W. Phelps, and others, from Kirtland, Ohio, 30 March 1834; *PWJS*, 317.

[2]Letter to Hezekiah Peck, from Kirtland, Ohio, 31 August 1835; *PWJS*, 346.

[3]Discourse of 26 May 1842, recorded by Eliza R. Snow; *WJS*, 121.

[4]Discourse of 10 March 1844, recorded by Wilford Woodruff; *WJS*, 331.

1 Kings

1 Kings 3:5–12

If we seek first the kingdom of God, all good things will be added. So [it was] with Solomon. First he asked wisdom, and God gave it him—and with it every desire of his heart.[1]

1 Kings 19:11–12

God is in the still small voice.[2]

---

[1]Letter to Nancy Rigdon, 1842, *Sangamo Journal,* 19 August 1842; *PWJS,* 508.

[2]Discourse of 26 May 1844, recorded by Thomas Bullock; *WJS,* 373.

1 Chronicles

1 Chronicles 13:7–10
See under 2 Samuel 6:2–7.

2 Chronicles

2 Chronicles 1:7–12

See under 1 Kings 3:5–12.

Esther

Esther 3–7

We want you to remember Haman and Mordecai. You know that Haman could not be satisfied so long as he saw Mordecai at the king's gate, and he sought the life of Mordecai and the people of the Jews. But the Lord so ordered that Haman was hanged upon his own gallows. So shall it come to pass with poor Haman in the last days. Those who have sought by their unbelief and wickedness and by the principle of mobocracy to destroy us and the people of God, by killing and scattering them abroad and wilfully and maliciously delivering us into the hands of murderers desiring us to be put to death, thereby having us dragged about in chains and cast into prison—and for what cause? It is because we were honest men and were determined to defend the lives of the Saints at the expense of our own. I say unto you that those who have thus vilely treated us like Haman shall be hanged upon their own gallows, or, in other words, shall fall into their own gin and trap and ditch, which they have prepared for us, and shall go backward and stumble and fall. And their names shall be blotted out, and God shall reward them according to all their abominations.[1]

---

[1]Letter to the Church in Caldwell County, from Liberty Jail, Missouri, 16 December 1838; *PWJS*, 375.

Job

Job 2:11

God suffered such kind of beings to afflict Job, but it never entered into their hearts that Job would get out of it all.[1]

Job 4–37

It is an unhallowed principle to say that such and such have transgressed because they have been preyed upon by disease or death, for all flesh is subject to death, and the Savior has said, "Judge not, lest ye be judged" [Matt. 7:1].[2]

In the book is a great display of human nature. It is very natural for a man when he sees his fellow man afflicted—his natural conclusion is that he is suffering the wrath of an angry God and turn from him in haste, not knowing the purpose of God.[3]

Job 38:4

The spirit or the intelligence of men are self-existent principles before the foundation [of] this earth. "Where wast thou when I laid the foundation of the earth?" [This is] evidence that Job was existing somewhere at that time.[4]

---

[1]Letter to the Church in Caldwell County, from Liberty Jail, Missouri, 16 December 1838; *PWJS*, 376.

[2]Discourse of 29 September 1839, recorded by James Mulholland; *PJS*, 2:332.

[3]Discourse of 28 March 1841, recorded by William P. McIntire; *WJS*, 67–68.

[4]Discourse of 28 March 1841, recorded by William P. McIntire; *WJS*, 68.

Psalms

Psalm 14:1

I looked upon the sun, the glorious luminary of the earth, and also the moon, rolling in their majesty through the heavens, and also the stars shining in their courses, and the earth also upon which I stood, and the beast of the field and the fowls of heaven and the fish of the waters, and also man walking forth upon the face of the earth in majesty and in the strength of beauty, whose power and intelligence in governing the things which are so exceeding great and marvelous [are] even in the likeness of him who created them. And when I considered upon these things my heart exclaimed, "Well hath the wise man said, 'It is a fool that saith in his heart there is no God.'" My heart exclaimed, "All these bear testimony and bespeak an omnipotent and omnipresent power, a being who maketh laws and decreeth and bindeth all things in their bounds, who filleth eternity, who was and is and will be from all eternity to eternity."[1]

Psalm 16:10

See under 2 Samuel 12:7–13; Acts 2:25–30.

Psalm 37:1–2

Don't envy sinners—have mercy on them; God will destroy them.[2]

God will see to it.[3]

Psalm 37:11

See under Matthew 5:5.

---

[1]1832 History; *PJS,* 1:6.
[2]Discourse of 28 April 1842, recorded by Eliza R. Snow; *WJS,* 118.
[3]Discourse of 26 May 1842, recorded by Eliza R. Snow; *WJS,* 121.

Psalm 53:1

See under Psalm 14:1.

Psalm 102:13–21

The city of Zion, spoken of by David in the 102nd psalm, will be built upon the land of America, and the ransomed of the Lord shall return and come to it with songs and everlasting joy upon their heads. And then they will be delivered from the overflowing scourge that shall pass through the land. But Judah shall obtain deliverance at Jerusalem.[4]

Psalm 133:1

It is very satisfactory to my mind that there has been such a good understanding existing between you, and that the Saints have so cheerfully hearkened to counsel and vied with each other in their labors of love and in the promotion of truth and righteousness. This is as it should be in the Church of Jesus Christ. Unity is strength. "How pleasant it is for brethren to dwell together in unity." Let the Saints of the Most High ever cultivate this principle and the most glorious blessings must result, not only to them individually but to the whole Church. The order of the kingdom will be maintained, its officers respected, and its requirements readily and cheerfully obeyed. Love is one of the leading characteristics of Deity and ought to be manifested by those who aspire to be the sons of God. A man filled with the love of God is not content with blessing his family alone but ranges through the world, anxious to bless the whole of the human family.[5]

---

[4]Letter to the editor, *American Revivalist and Rochester Observer,* from Kirtland, Ohio, 4 January 1833; *PWJS,* 273.

[5]Letter to the Twelve in Britain, from Nauvoo, Illinois, 15 December 1840; *PWJS,* 481.

Psalm 137:1–4

When the children of Zion are strangers in a strange land, their harps must be hung upon the willows. And they cannot sing the songs of Zion but should mourn and not dance. Therefore, brethren, it remains for all such to be exercised with prayer and continual supplication, until Zion is redeemed.[6]

---

[6]Letter to Hezekiah Peck, from Kirtland, Ohio, 31 August 1835; *PWJS*, 347.

Proverbs

Proverbs 16:18

Beware of pride also, for well and truly hath the wise man said that "pride goeth before destruction and a haughty spirit before a fall." And again, outward appearance is not always a criterion for us to judge our fellow man, but the lips betray the haughty and overbearing imaginations of the heart. By his words and his deeds let him be scanned.[1]

We would likewise say, beware of pride, for truly hath the wise man said, "Pride goeth before destruction, and an haughty spirit before a fall." Outward appearance is not always a criterion for us to judge our fellow man by, but the lips frequently betray the haughty and overbearing mind.[2]

---

[1]Letter to the Church at Quincy, Illinois, from Liberty Jail, Missouri, 20 March 1839; *PWJS*, 396. The verb *scan* in Joseph Smith's day meant "to examine with critical care; to scrutinize"; Noah Webster, *An American Dictionary of the English Language* (New York: S. Converse, 1828), s.v. "scan."

[2]*Times and Seasons*, May 1840, 102.

Isaiah

Isaiah 2:2–3

The Book of Mormon is a record of the forefathers of our western tribes of Indians. . . . By it we learn that our western tribes of Indians are descendants from that Joseph that was sold into Egypt, and that the land of America is a promised land unto them. And unto it all the tribes of Israel will come, with as many of the Gentiles as shall comply with the requisitions of the new covenant. But the tribe of Judah will return to old Jerusalem.[1]

The land of Zion consists of all North and South America. But any place where the Saints gather is Zion, which every righteous man will build up for a place of safety for his children.[2]

The Lord will begin by revealing the house of Israel among the Gentiles. And those who have gone from the ordinances of God shall return unto the keeping of all the law and observing his judgments and statutes to do them. Then shall the law of the Lord go forth from Zion and the word of the Lord to the priests, and through them from Jerusalem.[3]

I have another revelation, a great, grand, and glorious revelation. This is what I am going to declare. You know there has been great discussion where Zion is. . . . The whole America is [Zion] itself, North and South, and is described by the prophets that it should be in the center of the land. The declaration is that as soon as the temple and baptismal font are prepared, so we can wash and anoint the elders of Israel, . . . the elders of Israel shall build

---

[1]Letter to the editor, *American Revivalist and Rochester Observer*, from Kirtland, Ohio, 4 January 1833; *PWJS*, 273.

[2]Discourse of uncertain date, perhaps 19 July 1840, recorded by Martha Jane Coray; *WJS*, 415; see 418–19 n. 1 for a discussion of the date.

[3]Discourse of 21 March 1841, recorded by Martha Jane Coray; *WJS*, 67.

churches unto the Lord. And [wherever] they build churches unto the Lord, there shall be a stake of Zion. It is a glorious proclamation, and I reserved it to the last and design it to be understood, that it shall be after the washing and anointing here.[4]

[There] has been great discourse in relation to Zion. . . . [I] make a proclamation that will cover a broad ground. The whole America is Zion itself, from North to South. That is the Zion where the mountain of the Lord should be. [As] soon as [the] temple [is] finished—washing, anointing, etc.—when those last and most important ordinances can be done, . . . from henceforth I have received instruction from [the] Lord that [the] elders shall build churches wherever they raise branches through the States. Then build stakes. In the great cities—Boston, etc.—there shall be stakes. [I] reserved the proclamation to the last. All this [is] to be understood, that this work shall commence after the washing, anointing, and endowment here.[5]

I have another great and grand revelation, [a] great discussion where Zion is. The whole America is Zion. That is the Zion where the mountain of the Lord's house shall be, about the central part of North and South America. [As] soon as the temple is finished, . . . from henceforth the elders shall build churches wherever the people receive the gospel sufficiently. Then build stakes to this place.[6]

I have now a great proclamation for the elders to teach the Church hereafter, which is in relation to Zion. The whole of North and South America is Zion. The mountain of the Lord's house is in the center of North and South America. When the house is done, [the] baptismal font erected and finished, and the

---

[4]Discourse of 8 April 1844, recorded by Thomas Bullock; *WJS,* 364.

[5]Discourse of 8 April 1844, recorded by William Clayton; *WJS,* 362–63.

[6]Discourse of 8 April 1844, recorded by Willard Richards; *WJS,* 365.

worthy are washed, anointed, endowed, and ordained kings and priests, . . . then the elders are to go through all America and build up churches, until all Zion is built up. But [they are] not to commence to do this until the temple is built up here and the elders endowed. Then go forth and accomplish the work and build up stakes in all North and South America.[7]

Isaiah 2:4

The government of the Almighty has always been very dissimilar to the government of men, whether we refer to his religious government or to the government of nations. The government of God has always tended to promote peace, unity, harmony, strength, and happiness, while that of man has been productive of confusion, disorder, weakness, and misery. The greatest acts of the mighty men have been to depopulate nations and to overthrow kingdoms. And whilst they have exalted themselves and become glorious, it has been at the expense of the lives of the innocent, the blood of the oppressed, the moans of the widow, and the tears of the orphan. Egypt, Babylon, Greece, Persia, Carthage, and Rome—each was raised to dignity amid the clash of arms and the din of war. And whilst their triumphant leaders led forth their victorious armies to glory and victory, their ears were saluted with the groans of the dying and the misery and distress of the human family. "Before them the earth was a paradise, and behind them a desolate wilderness" [Joel 2:3]. Their kingdoms were founded in carnage and bloodshed and sustained by oppression, tyranny, and despotism.

The designs of God have been to promote the universal good of the universal world, to establish peace and good will among men, to promote the principles of eternal truth, to bring about a state of things that shall unite man to his fellow man, cause the world to "beat their swords into plowshares, and their spears into pruninghooks," make the nations of the earth dwell in peace, and

---

[7]Discourse of 8 April 1844, recorded by Wilford Woodruff; *WJS,* 363–64.

to bring about the millennial glory when the earth shall yield its increase, resume its paradisean glory, and become as the garden of the Lord. . . .

Monarchial, aristocratic, and republican forms of government, of their various kinds and grades, have, in their turn, been raised to dignity and prostrated in the dust. The plans of the greatest politicians, the wisest senators, and [the] most profound statesmen have been exploded. And the proceedings of the greatest chieftains, the bravest generals, and the wisest kings have fallen to the ground. Nation has succeeded nation, and we have inherited nothing but their folly. History records their puerile plans, their short-lived glory, their feeble intellect, and their ignoble deeds. . . . All speak with a voice of thunder that man is not able to govern himself, to legislate for himself, to protect himself, [nor] to promote his own good nor the good of the world.

It has been the design of Jehovah from the commencement of the world, and is his purpose now, to regulate the affairs of the world in his own time, to stand as head of the universe and take the reigns of government into his own hand. When that is done, judgment will be administered in righteousness, anarchy and confusion will be destroyed, and "nations will learn war no more." . . .

Other attempts to promote universal peace and happiness in the human family have proven abortive. Every effort has failed; every plan and design has fallen to the ground. It needs the wisdom of God, the intelligence of God, and the power of God to accomplish this.

The world has had a fair trial for six thousand years. The Lord will try the seventh thousand himself. He whose right it is will possess the kingdom and "reign, until he has put all things under his feet" [1 Cor. 15:25].[8]

---

[8]*Times and Seasons,* 15 July 1842, 855–57.

Isaiah 11:4

I mourn for the depravity of the world. . . . I long for a day of righteousness when he whose right it is to reign shall "judge the poor, and reprove with equity for the meek of the earth." And I pray God, who hath given our fathers a promise of a perfect government in the last days, to purify the hearts of the people and hasten the welcome day.[9]

Isaiah 11:11

The time has at last arrived when the God of Abraham, of Isaac, and of Jacob has set his hand again the second time to recover the remnants of his people which have been left from Assyria, and from Egypt, and from Pathros, and from the islands of the sea, and with them to bring in the fulness of the Gentiles and establish that covenant with them which was promised when their sins should be taken away.[10]

Isaiah 24:5

Who can look at [the world] and not exclaim in the language of Isaiah, "The earth is defiled under the inhabitants thereof; because they have transgressed the laws, changed the ordinances, and broken the everlasting covenant"?

The plain fact is this: the power of God begins to fall upon the nations, and the light of the latter-day glory begins to break forth through the dark atmosphere of sectarian wickedness, and their iniquity rolls up into view. And the nations of the Gentiles are like the waves of the sea, casting up mire and dirt, or all in commotion. And they hastily are preparing to act the part allotted them when the Lord rebukes the nations, when he shall rule them with

---

[9]*Times and Seasons,* 1 June 1844, 547–48.

[10]Letter to the editor, *American Revivalist and Rochester Observer,* from Kirtland, Ohio, 4 January 1833; *PWJS,* 271.

a rod of iron and break them in pieces like a potters vessel. The Lord has declared to his servants some eighteen months since that he was then withdrawing his Spirit from the earth, and we can see that such is the fact. For not only the churches are dwindling away, but there are no conversions, or but very few. And this is not all. The governments of the earth are thrown into confusion and division, and destruction to the eye of the spiritual beholder seems to be written by the finger of an invisible hand in large capitals upon almost everything we behold.

And now what remains to be done under circumstances like these? I will proceed to tell you what the Lord requires of all people—high and low, rich and poor, male and female, ministers and people, professors of religion and nonprofessors—in order that they may enjoy the Holy Spirit of God to a fulness and escape the judgments of God which are almost ready to burst upon the nations of the earth: Repent of all your sins and be baptized in water for the remission of them, in the name of the Father, and of the Son, and of the Holy Ghost. And receive the ordinance of the laying on of the hands of him who is ordained and sealed unto this power, that ye may receive the Holy Spirit of God.[11]

Isaiah 24:21–22

Thus we find that God will deal with all the human family equally, and that as the antediluvians had their day of visitation [1 Pet. 3:19–20], so will those characters referred to by Isaiah have their time of visitation and deliverance, after having been many days in prison. . . . [They] will be visited by this priesthood and come out of their prison, upon the same principle as those who were disobedient in the days of Noah were visited by our Savior.[12]

See also under 1 Peter 3:18–19; 4:6.

---

[11]Letter to the editor, *American Revivalist and Rochester Observer,* from Kirtland, Ohio, 4 January 1833; *PWJS,* 272–73.

[12]*Times and Seasons,* 15 April 1842, 760.

Isaiah 29:11–12; Isaiah 29:20–22, JST
(2 Nephi 27:15–20)

The Lord had shown [Martin Harris] that he must go to New York City with some of the characters, so we proceeded to copy some of them. And he took his journey to the eastern cities and to the learned, saying, "Read this, I pray thee." And the learned said, "I cannot," but if he would bring the plates they would read it. But the Lord had forbidden it. And he returned to me and gave them to me to translate, and I said, "[I] cannot, for I am not learned." But the Lord had prepared spectacles for to read the book, therefore I commenced translating the characters, and thus the prophecy of Isaiah was fulfilled.[13]

Isaiah 29:21

We believe the old prophet verily told the truth.[14]

Isaiah 33:14

God Almighty himself dwells in eternal fire. Flesh and blood cannot go there, for all corruption is devoured by the fire. Our God is a consuming fire. When our flesh is quickened by the Spirit, there will be no blood in the tabernacles. Some dwell in higher glory than others. Those who have done wrong always have that wrong gnawing them. Immortality dwells in everlasting burnings. . . . All men who are immortal dwell in everlasting burnings.[15]

God dwells in flaming flames, and he is a consuming fire. He will consume all that is unclean and unholy, and we could not abide his presence unless pure spirit is in us.[16]

---

[13]1832 History; *PJS,* 1:9.

[14]Letter to the Church in Caldwell County, from Liberty Jail, Missouri, 16 December 1838; *PWJS,* 376.

[15]Discourse of 12 May 1844, recorded by Thomas Bullock; *WJS,* 368–69.

[16]Discourse of 12 May 1844, recorded by George Laub; *WJS,* 371.

All resurrected bodies dwell in flaming fire, for our God is a consuming fire.[17]

Isaiah 42:7

See under 1 Peter 3:18–19; 4:6.

Isaiah 51:3

We must wait patiently until the Lord comes and restores unto us all things and builds the waste places again. For he will do it in his time.[18]

O God, I ask thee in the name of Jesus of Nazareth to save all things concerning Zion and build up her waste places and restore all things. O God, send forth judgement unto victory. Oh come down and cause the mountains to flow down at thy presence![19]

I feel to cry mightily unto the Lord, . . . yea I feel to say, "O Lord, let Zion be comforted, let her waste places be built up and established an hundred fold. Let thy Saints come unto Zion out of every nation, let her be exalted to the third heaven, and let thy judgments be sent forth unto victory. And after this great tribulation, let thy blessings fall upon thy people."[20]

Isaiah 51:11

See under Psalm 102:13–21.

---

[17]Discourse of 12 May 1844, recorded by Samuel W. Richards; *WJS,* 372.

[18]Letter to W. W. Phelps, John Whitmer, Edward Partridge, Isaac Morley, John Corrill, and Sidney Gilbert, 18 August 1833; *PWJS,* 286.

[19]Letter to W. W. Phelps, John Whitmer, Edward Partridge, Isaac Morley, John Corrill, and Sidney Gilbert, 18 August 1833; *PWJS,* 288.

[20]Letter to Vienna Jacques, from Kirtland, Ohio, 4 September 1833; *PWJS,* 295.

Isaiah 52:1–2

Notwithstanding her present affliction, [Zion] shall yet arise and put on her beautiful garments, and be the joy and glory of the whole earth.[21]

I know that Zion, in the own due time of the Lord, will be redeemed. But how many will be the days of her purification, tribulation, and affliction, the Lord has kept hid from my eyes. And when I inquire concerning this subject, the voice of the Lord is, "Be still, and know that I am God! All those who suffer for my name shall reign with me, and he that layeth down his life for my sake shall find it again." Now there are two things of which I am ignorant and the Lord will not show me, perhaps for a wise purpose in himself . . . : Why God hath suffered so great [a] calamity to come upon Zion, or what the great moving cause of this great affliction is; and again, by what means he will return her back to her inheritance with songs of everlasting joy upon her head. These two things, brethren, are in part kept back that they are not plainly shown unto me.[22]

Isaiah 52:8

I arrived in Jackson County, Missouri, and after viewing the country, seeking diligently at the hand of God, he manifested himself unto me and designated to me and others the very spot upon which he designed to commence the work of the gathering and the upbuilding of a holy city which should be called Zion— Zion, because it is to be a place of righteousness, and all who build thereon are to worship the true and living God and all

---

[21]Letter to Vienna Jacques, from Kirtland, Ohio, 4 September 1833; *PWJS*, 295.

[22]Letter to Edward Partridge, W. W. Phelps, John Whitmer, Algernon Sidney Gilbert, John Corrill, Isaac Morley, and all the Saints whom it may concern, from Kirtland Mills, Ohio, 10 December 1833; *PWJS*, 308–9.

believe in one doctrine, even the doctrine of our Lord and Savior Jesus Christ.[23]

If all the world should embrace this gospel, they would then see eye to eye, and the blessings of God would be poured out upon the people.[24]

Isaiah 60:2

Consider for a moment, brethren, the fulfillment of the words of the prophet. For we behold that darkness covers the earth and gross darkness the minds of the inhabitants thereof, that crimes of every description are increasing among men, vices of every enormity are practiced, the rising generation growing up in the fulness of pride and arrogance, the aged losing every sense of conviction and seemingly banishing every thought of a day of retribution; intemperance, immorality, extravagance, pride, blindness of heart, idolatry, the loss of natural affection, the love of this world and indifference toward the things of eternity increasing among those who profess a belief in the religion of heaven, and infidelity spreading itself in consequence of the same, men giving themselves up to commit acts of the foulest kind and deeds of the blackest dye, lying, blaspheming, stealing, robbing, murdering, defaming, defrauding, blasting the reputation of neighbors, advocating error and opposing the truth, forsaking the covenant of heaven, and denying the faith of Jesus.[25]

Isaiah 60:13–17

The prophets have said concerning Zion in the last days [that] the glory of Lebanon is to come upon her, the fir tree, the pine tree, and the box together, to beautify the place of [God's]

---

[23]*Messenger and Advocate,* September 1835, 179.

[24]Discourse of 22 January 1843, recorded by Wilford Woodruff; *WJS,* 159.

[25]*Evening and Morning Star,* February 1834, 135.

sanctuary that he may make the place of his feet glorious, where for brass he will bring gold, and for iron he will bring silver, and for wood brass, and for stones iron, and where the feast of fat things will be given to the just. Yea, when the splendor of the Lord is brought to our consideration for the good of his people, the calculations of men and the vain glory of the world vanishes, and we exclaim, "God will shine the perfection of beauty out of Zion" [Ps. 50:2].[26]

Isaiah 64:1

See under Isaiah 51:3.

---

[26]1839 History; *PJS,* 1:360.

Jeremiah

Jeremiah 31:31–33

This covenant has never been established with the house of Israel, nor with the house of Judah. For it requires two parties to make a covenant, and those two parties must be agreed or no covenant can be made. Christ in the days of his flesh proposed to make a covenant with them, but they rejected him and his proposals. And in consequence thereof they were broken off, and no covenant was made with them at that time. But their unbelief has not rendered the promise of God of none effect. No, for there was another day limited in David which was the day of his power. And then his people, Israel, should be a willing people, and he would write his laws in their hearts and print them in their thoughts. Their sins and their iniquities he would remember no more.[1]

Jeremiah 31:34

The day must come when no man need say to his neighbor, "Know ye the Lord." For all shall know him (who remain), from the least to the greatest. How is this to be done? It is to be done by this sealing power and the Other Comforter spoken of, which will be manifested by revelation.[2]

---

[1] Letter to the editor, *American Revivalist and Rochester Observer,* from Kirtland, Ohio, 4 January 1833; *PWJS,* 271.

[2] Discourse of 27 June 1839, recorded in Willard Richards's "Pocket Companion"; *WJS,* 4.

Ezekiel

Ezekiel 14:13–20

The Lord had declared by the prophet that the people should each one stand for himself and depend on no man or men in that state of corruption of the Jewish church—that righteous persons could only deliver their own souls. [This applies] to the present state of the Church of Latter-day Saints. If the people depart from the Lord they must fall. They are depending on the prophet [and] hence are darkened in their minds from neglect of themselves, envious toward the innocent, while they afflict the virtuous with their shafts of envy.[1]

Ezekiel 32:17–32

The old Pharaoh was comforted and greatly rejoiced that he was honored as a kind of King Devil over those uncircumcised nations that go down to hell for rejecting the word of the Lord, withstanding his mighty miracles, and fighting the Saints. The whole [is] exhibited as a pattern to this generation and the nations now rolling in splendor over the globe—if they do not repent—that they shall go down to the pit also, and be rejoiced over and ruled over by old Pharaoh, King Devil of mobocrats, miracle rejecters, Saint killers, hypocritical priests, and all other fit subjects, to fester in their own infamy.[2]

Ezekiel 34:11–13

These are testimonies that the Good Shepherd will put forth his own sheep and lead them out from all nations where they

---

[1]Discourse of 26 May 1842, recorded by Eliza R. Snow; *WJS*, 120.
[2]Discourse of 5 June 1842, recorded in *The Wasp; WJS*, 122.

have been scattered in a cloudy and dark day, to Zion and to Jerusalem.[3]

Ezekiel 37:19

The Book of Mormon [is] the Stick of Joseph in the hands of Ephraim.[4]

Ezekiel 47:1, 8

Jerusalem must be rebuilt, and Judah must return. And the temple, water [will] come out from under the temple. The waters of the Dead Sea [will] be healed. It will take some time to build the walls and the temple.[5]

---

[3]Letter to the editor, *American Revivalist and Rochester Observer,* from Kirtland, Ohio, 4 January 1833; *PWJS,* 273.

[4]1839 History; *PJS,* 1:307.

[5]Discourse of 6 April 1843, recorded by Willard Richards; *WJS,* 180.

Daniel

Daniel 2:44

May God enable us all to perform our vows and covenants with each other in all fidelity and righteousness before him, that our influence may be felt among the nations of the earth in mighty power, even to rend the kingdom of darkness in sunder and triumph over priestcraft and spiritual wickedness in high places, and break in pieces all kingdoms that are opposed to the kingdom of Christ, and spread the light and truth of the everlasting gospel from the rivers to the ends of the earth.[1]

The kingdom will not be broken up, but we shall be scattered and driven, gathered again, and then dispersed, reestablished, driven abroad, and so on, until the Ancient of Days shall sit. And the kingdom and power thereof shall then be given to the Saints, and they shall possess it forever and ever, which may God hasten for Christ's sake.[2]

I calculate to be one of the instruments of setting up the kingdom [spoken of by] Daniel, by the word of the Lord. And I intend to lay a foundation that will revolutionize the whole world. . . . It will not be by sword or gun that this kingdom will roll on. The power of truth is such that all nations will be under the necessity of obeying the gospel.[3]

Daniel 7:1–8

The prophets do not declare that they saw a beast or beasts, but that they saw the image or figure of a beast. They did not see an actual bear or lion, but the images or figures of those beasts.

---

[1] Journal, 16 January 1836; *PJS*, 2:148; cf. *PJS*, 1:206.

[2] Discourse of 21 March 1841, recorded by Martha Jane Coray; *WJS*, 67.

[3] Discourse of 12 May 1844, recorded by Thomas Bullock; *WJS*, 367.

The translation should have been rendered "image" instead of "beast" in every instance where beasts are mentioned by the prophets.[4]

By [the] figure of beasts, God represented the kingdoms of the world. [The] bear, lion, etc. represented the kingdoms of the world. . . . Daniel did not see a lion and a bear. He saw an image like unto a bear.[5]

See also under Daniel 7:15–24.

Daniel 7:9–14

Spring Hill [was] a name appropriated by the brethren present. But afterwards [it was] named by the mouth of [the] Lord and was called Adam-ondi-Ahman, because, said he, it is the place where Adam shall come to visit his people, or the Ancient of Days shall sit, as spoken of by Daniel the prophet.[6]

Daniel speaks of the Ancient of Days; he means the oldest man, our Father Adam, Michael. He will call his children together and hold a council with them to prepare them for the coming of the Son of Man. He (Adam) is the father of the human family and presides over the spirits of all men, and all that have had the keys must stand before him in this great council. This may take place before some of us leave this stage of action. The Son of Man stands before him and there is given him glory and dominion. Adam delivers up his stewardship to Christ, that which was delivered to him as holding the keys of the universe, but retains his standing as head of the human family. . . .

---

[4]Discourse of 8 April 1843, recorded by William Clayton; *WJS*, 185.

[5]Discourse of 8 April 1843, recorded by Willard Richards; *WJS*, 188.

[6]Statement of 19 May 1838, recorded by George W. Robinson; *PJS*, 2:244–45; see D&C 116.

Those men to whom these keys have been given will have to be there; they without us cannot be made perfect [Heb. 11:40]. These men are in heaven, but their children are on earth. Their bowels yearn over us. . . . All these authoritative characters will come down and join hand in hand in bringing about this work. . . . We cannot be made perfect without them, nor they without us. When these things are done, the Son of Man will descend [and] the Ancient of Days sit. We may come to an innumerable company of angels [and] have communion with and receive instruction from them.[7]

This then is the nature of the priesthood, every man holding the presidency of his dispensation and one man holding the presidency of them all, even Adam, and Adam receiving his presidency and authority from Christ. But [he] cannot receive a fulness until Christ shall present the kingdom to the Father, which shall be at the end of the last dispensation.[8]

See also under Genesis 1:26–28a.

Daniel 7:15–24

God never made use of the figure of a beast to represent the kingdom of heaven. When they were made use of, it was to represent an apostate church.[9]

When God made use of the figure of a beast in visions to the prophets, he did it to represent those kingdoms who had degenerated and become corrupt—the kingdoms of the world. But he never made use of the figure of a beast nor any of the brute kind to represent his kingdom. Daniel says when he saw the vision of

---

[7]Discourse of summer of 1839, recorded in Willard Richards's "Pocket Companion"; *WJS*, 8–9, 10.

[8]Discourse of 5 October 1840, recorded by Robert B. Thompson; *WJS*, 40.

[9]Discourse of 2 April 1843, recorded by William Clayton; *WJS*, 170–71.

the four beasts, "I came near unto one of them that stood by, and asked him the truth of all this." The angel interpreted the vision to Daniel. But we find by the interpretation that the figures of beasts had no allusion to the kingdom of God. You there see that the beasts are spoken of to represent the kingdoms of the world, the inhabitants whereof were beastly and abominable characters. They were murderous, corrupt, carnivorous, and brutal in their dispositions.[10]

A beast is never used to represent the Church, but man in his degenerate state, having become like brute beasts.[11]

Daniel 7:27

See under Daniel 2:44.

Daniel 12:3

It is for us to be righteous, that we may be wise and understand.[12]

---

[10]Discourse of 8 April 1843, recorded by William Clayton; *WJS,* 184.

[11]Discourse of 8 April 1843, recorded by Franklin D. Richards; *WJS,* 190.

[12]*Times and Seasons,* 15 July 1842, 857.

Joel

Joel 2:30–31

The prophecies must be fulfilled: [the] sun [will] be turned into darkness, [the] moon into blood, and many more things before Christ comes.[1]

See also under Matthew 24:27–30.

Joel 3:18

See under Ezekiel 47:1, 8.

---

[1]Statement of 12 February 1843, recorded by Willard Richards; *PJS*, 3.

Amos

Amos 3:7

The grand rule of heaven was that nothing should ever be done on earth without revealing the secret to his servants the prophets.[1]

The prophet says that God will do nothing but what he will reveal unto his servants the prophets. Consequently, if it is not made known to the prophets, it will not come to pass.[2]

---

[1]*Times and Seasons,* 1 September 1842, 905.

[2]Discourse of 6 April 1843, recorded by James Burgess; *WJS,* 181.

Micah

Micah 4:1–2

See under Isaiah 2:2–3.

Micah 4:3

See under Isaiah 2:4.

Zechariah

Zechariah 14:8

See under Ezekiel 47:1, 8.

Zechariah 14:16–19

The wicked[1] will not all be destroyed at the coming of Christ, and there will be wicked during the Millennium. . . . That Jesus will be a resident on the earth a thousand [years] with the Saints is not the case, but [he] will reign over the Saints and come down and instruct, as he did the five hundred brethren [1 Cor. 15:6]. Those of the first resurrection will also reign with him over the Saints.[2]

Christ and the resurrected Saints will reign over the earth but not dwell on the earth. [They will] visit it when they please or when necessary to govern it. There will be wicked men on the earth during the one thousand years. The heathen nations who will not come up to worship will be destroyed.[3]

---

[1]Elder Joseph Fielding Smith explained: "The Prophet's statement that there will be wicked men on the earth during the Millennium has caused considerable confusion in the minds of many who have read in the Scripture in many places that when Christ comes the earth shall be cleansed from its wickedness, and that the wicked shall not stand, but shall be consumed. . . . In using the term 'wicked men,' . . . the Prophet did so in the same sense in which the Lord uses it in the eighty-fourth section of the Doctrine and Covenants, [verses] 49-53. The Lord in this scripture speaks of those who have not received the Gospel as being under the bondage of sin, and hence 'wicked.' However, many of these people are honorable, clean-living men, but they have not embraced the Gospel. The inhabitants of the terrestrial order will remain on the earth during the Millennium, and this class are without the Gospel ordinances." Joseph Smith, *Teachings of the Prophet Joseph Smith,* sel. Joseph Fielding Smith (Salt Lake City: Deseret Book, 1938), 268–69.

[2]Statement of 16 March 1841, recorded by William P. McIntire; *WJS,* 65.

[3]Statement of 30 December 1842, recorded by Willard Richards; *PJS,* 3.

Malachi

Malachi 3:2–4

The Lord will purify the sons of Levi, good or bad, for it is through them that blessings flow to Israel. And as Israel once was baptized in the cloud and in the sea, so shall God as a refiner's fire and a fuller's soap purify the sons of Levi and purge them as gold and as silver. And then, and not till then, "shall the offering of Judah and Jerusalem be pleasant unto the Lord, as in days of old, and as in former years."[1]

The purifying of the sons of Levi is by giving unto them intelligence.[2]

Malachi 3:3

The offering of sacrifice also shall be continued at the last time, for all the ordinances and duties that ever have been required by the priesthood under the direction and commandments of the Almighty, in any of the dispensations, shall all be had in the last dispensation. Therefore, all things had under the authority of the priesthood at any former period shall be had again—bringing to pass the restoration spoken of by the mouth of all the holy prophets. Then shall the sons of Levi offer an acceptable sacrifice to the Lord.

It will be necessary here to make a few observations on the doctrine set forth in [this passage], as it is generally supposed that sacrifice was entirely done away when the great sacrifice was offered up and that there will be no necessity for the ordinance of sacrifice in [the] future. But those who assert this are certainly not acquainted with the duties, privileges, and authority of the priesthood, or with the prophets. The offering of sacrifice has ever been

---

[1]Discourse of 21 March 1841, recorded by Martha Jane Coray; *WJS,* 66.

[2]Statement of 28 December 1842, recorded by Willard Richards; *PJS,* 3.

connected [with], and forms a part of, the duties of the priesthood. It began with the priesthood and will be continued until after the coming of Christ, from generation to generation. We frequently have mention made of the offering of sacrifice by the servants of the Most High in ancient days prior to the law of Moses, which ordinances will be continued when the priesthood is restored with all its authority, power, and blessings. . . .

These sacrifices as well as every ordinance belonging to the priesthood will, when the temple of the Lord shall be built and the sons [of] Levi be purified, be fully restored and attended to then, [with] all their powers, ramifications, and blessings. This ever was and will exist when the powers of the Melchizedek Priesthood are sufficiently manifested. Else how can the restitution of all things spoken of by all the holy prophets be brought to pass? It is not to be understood that the law of Moses will be established again with all its rites and variety of ceremonies; this had never been spoken of by the prophets. But those things which existed prior [to] Moses' day, namely sacrifice, will be continued. It may be asked by some what necessity [there is] for sacrifice, since the great sacrifice was offered. In answer to [this], if repentance, baptism, and faith existed prior to the days of Christ, what necessity [is there] for them since that time?[3]

Malachi 3:5

He shall witness against all iniquity, as said Malachi, and shall sorely chastise those who are gone astray.[4]

Malachi 4:1

The world is reserved unto burning in the last days.[5]

---

[3]Discourse of 5 October 1840, recorded by Robert B. Thompson; *WJS*, 42-44.

[4]Discourse of 21 March 1841, recorded by Martha Jane Coray; *WJS*, 66.

[5]Discourse of 13 August 1843, recorded by Willard Richards; *WJS*, 239.

Malachi 4:4

[The] law revealed to Moses in Horeb never was revealed to the children of Israel.[6]

Malachi 4:5–6

The hearts of the children will have to be turned to the fathers, and the fathers to the children, living or dead, to prepare them for the coming of the Son of Man. If Elijah did not come, the whole earth would be smitten.[7]

Elijah was the last prophet that held the keys of this priesthood, and who will, before the last dispensation, restore the authority and deliver the keys of this priesthood in order that all the ordinances may be attended to in righteousness. It is true that the Savior had authority and power to bestow this blessing, but the sons of Levi were too prejudiced. Why send Elijah? Because he holds the keys of the authority to administer in all the ordinances of the priesthood. And without the authority given, the ordinances could not be administered in righteousness.[8]

[Malachi] had his eye fixed on the restoration of the priesthood, the glories to be revealed in the last days, and in an especial manner this most glorious of all subjects belonging to the everlasting gospel, namely, the baptism for the dead. . . . I might have rendered a plainer translation to this, but it is sufficiently plain to suit my purpose as it stands. It is sufficient to know, in this case, that the earth will be smitten with a curse unless there is a welding link of some kind or other between the fathers and the children, upon some subject or other—and behold what is that subject? It is the baptism for the dead. For we without them cannot be made perfect; neither can

---

[6]Discourse of 27 August 1843, recorded by Willard Richards; *WJS,* 244.

[7]Discourse of summer of 1839, recorded in Willard Richards's "Pocket Companion"; *WJS,* 11.

[8]Discourse of 5 October 1840, recorded by Robert B. Thompson; *WJS,* 43.

they without us be made perfect [Heb. 11:40]. Neither can they nor we be made perfect without those who have died in the gospel also.[9]

"And he shall turn the hearts of the children to the covenant made with their fathers."[10]

In the end [the earth] shall be burned and few men left. But before that, God shall send unto them Elijah the prophet, and he shall reveal unto them the covenants of the fathers with relation to the children and the covenants of the children in relation to the fathers, that they may have the privilege of entering into the same, in order to effect their mutual salvation.[11]

"I will send Elijah the prophet, and he shall reveal the covenants of the fathers to the children and of the children to the fathers, that they may enter into covenant with each other, lest I come and smite the whole earth with a curse."[12]

He shall send Elijah the prophet, and he shall reveal the covenants of the fathers in relation to the children, and the covenants of the children in relation to the fathers.[13]

How shall God come to the rescue of this generation? He shall send Elijah, . . . and he shall reveal the covenants to seal the hearts of the fathers to the children and the children to the fathers.[14]

Now the word "turn" here should be translated "bind" or "seal." But what is the object of this important mission, or how is

---

[9]*Times and Seasons,* 1 October 1842, 935; D&C 128:17–18.

[10]Discourse of 13 August 1843, recorded by William Clayton; *WJS,* 242.

[11]Discourse of 13 August 1843, recorded by Martha Jane Coray; *WJS,* 240.

[12]Discourse of 13 August 1843, recorded by Franklin D. Richards; *WJS,* 241.

[13]Discourse of 13 August 1843, recorded by Willard Richards; *WJS,* 239.

[14]Discourse of 27 August 1843, recorded by Willard Richards; *WJS,* 244.

it to be fulfilled? The keys are to be delivered, the spirit of Elijah is to come, the gospel to be established, the Saints of God gathered, Zion built up, and the Saints to come up as saviors on Mount Zion. But how are they to become saviors on Mount Zion? By building their temples, erecting their baptismal fonts, and going forth and receiving all the ordinances, baptisms, confirmations, washings, anointings, ordinations, and sealing powers upon our heads in behalf of all our progenitors who are dead, and redeem them that they may come forth in the first resurrection and be exalted to thrones of glory with us. And herein is the chain that binds the hearts of the fathers to the children, and the children to the fathers, which fulfills the mission of Elijah. . . .

The Saints have none too much time to save and redeem their dead and gather together their living relatives that they may be saved also, before the earth will be smitten and the consumption decreed falls upon the world. And I would advise all the Saints to go to with their might and gather together all their living relatives to this place, that they may be sealed and saved, that they may be prepared against the day that the destroying angel goes forth. And if the whole Church should go to with all their might to save their dead, seal their posterity, gather their living friends, and spend none of their time in behalf of the world, they would hardly get through before night would come, when no man could work. . . . The question is frequently asked, "Can we not be saved without going through with all these ordinances?" I would answer, "No, not the fulness of salvation."[15]

The spirit of Elijah is the sealing power, to seal the hearts of the fathers to the children and the children to the parents.[16]

The spirit of Elijah is that degree of power which holds the sealing power of the kingdom, to seal the hearts of the fathers to

---

[15]Discourse of 21 January 1844, recorded by Wilford Woodruff; *WJS,* 318–19.

[16]Discourse of 10 March 1844, recorded by Thomas Bullock; *WJS,* 336.

the children and of the children [to] their fathers—not only on earth but in heaven, both the living and the dead to each other. For they (the dead) cannot be made perfect without us [Heb. 11:40].[17]

The spirit, power, and calling of Elijah is that ye have power to hold the keys of the revelations, ordinances, oracles, powers, and endowments of the fulness of the Melchizedek Priesthood and of the kingdom of God on the earth, and to receive, obtain, and perform all the ordinances belonging to the kingdom of God, even unto the sealing of the hearts of the fathers unto the children and the hearts of the children unto the fathers, even those who are in heaven. Now what I am after is the knowledge of God, and I take my own course to obtain it. What are we to understand by this in the last days? In the days of Noah, God destroyed the world by a flood and has promised to destroy it by fire in the last days. But before it takes place, Elijah should first come and turn the hearts of the fathers to the children, and so forth. Now comes the point. What is this office and work of Elijah? It is one of the greatest and most important subjects that God has revealed. He should send Elijah to seal the children to the fathers and fathers to the children. Now was this merely confined to the living, to settle difficulties with families on earth? By no means; it was a far greater work. Elijah, what would you do if you were here? Would you confine your work to the living alone? No.

I would refer you to the scriptures where the subject is manifest: "Without us they could not be made perfect" [Heb. 11:40], nor we without them, the fathers without the children nor the children without the fathers. I wish you to understand this subject, for it is important, and if you will receive it, this is the spirit of Elijah: that we redeem our dead and connect ourselves with

---

[17]Discourse of 10 March 1844, recorded by Franklin D. Richards; *WJS,* 334.

our fathers, which are in heaven, and seal up our dead to come forth in the first resurrection. And here we want the power of Elijah to seal those who dwell on earth to those which dwell in heaven. This is the power of Elijah and the keys of the kingdom of Jehovah. Let us suppose a case. Suppose the great God who dwells in heaven should reveal himself to [a man] here by the opening heavens and tell him, "I offer up a decree that whatsoever you seal on earth with your decree I will seal it in heaven." You have power then. Can it be taken off? No. Then what you seal on earth by the keys of Elijah is sealed in heaven, and this is the power of Elijah. And this is the difference between the spirit and power of Elias and Elijah, for while the spirit of Elias is a forerunner, the power of Elijah is sufficient to make our calling and election sure. . . .

Again, the doctrine or sealing power of Elijah is as follows: If you have power to seal on earth and in heaven, then we should be crafty.[18] The first thing you do [is] go and seal on earth your sons and daughters unto yourself, and yourself unto your fathers in eternal glory, and go ahead and not go back. But use a little craftiness and seal all you can. And when you get to heaven, tell your father that what you seal on earth should be sealed in heaven. I will walk through the gate of heaven and claim what I seal and those that follow me and my counsel. . . .

Elias is a forerunner to prepare the way, and the spirit and power of Elijah is to come after—holding the keys of power, building the temple to the capstone, placing the seals of the Melchizedek Priesthood upon the house of Israel, and making all things ready. Then Messiah comes to his temple, which is last of all. Messiah is above the spirit and power of Elijah, for he made

---

[18]Among the definitions of *crafty* in Joseph Smith's day was "artful . . . in a good sense, or in a laudable pursuit"; Noah Webster, *An American Dictionary of the English Language* (New York: S. Converse, 1828), s.v. "crafty."

the world and was that spiritual rock unto Moses in the wilderness. Elijah was to come and prepare the way and build up the kingdom before the coming of the great day of the Lord, although the spirit of Elias might begin it.[19]

---

[19]Discourse of 10 March 1844, recorded by Wilford Woodruff; *WJS*, 329–30, 331–32.

Matthew

Matthew 3:1–6

Now it was written that the priests' lips should keep knowledge, and to them should the people seek for understanding [Mal. 2:7]. And above all, the law binds them and us to receive the word of the Lord at the hands of the Levites. Therefore, John being lawful heir to the Levitical Priesthood, the people were bound to receive his testimony.[1]

John was not a restorer but a forerunner.[2]

The kingdom of God was set upon the earth in all ages, from the days of Adam to the present time, whenever there was a man on earth who had authority to administer the ordinances of the gospel, or a priest of God. And unto such a man, God did reveal his will.[3]

Where the oracles of God are revealed, there is the kingdom of God. Wherever the oracles of God are and subjects to obey those oracles, there is the kingdom of God. What constitutes the kingdom of God? An administrator who has the power of calling down the oracles of God, and subjects to receive those oracles, no matter if there are but three, four, or six. There is the kingdom of God.[4]

Some say the kingdom of God was not set up on earth until the day of Pentecost and that John did not preach the baptism of repentance for the remission of sins. But I say in the name of the Lord that the kingdom of God was set up on earth from the days of Adam to the present time whenever there has been a righteous

---

[1]Discourse of 21 March 1841, recorded by Martha Jane Coray; *WJS*, 65.
[2]Discourse of 21 March 1841, recorded by Martha Jane Coray; *WJS*, 66.
[3]Discourse of 17 January 1843, recorded by Wilford Woodruff; *WJS*, 155.
[4]Discourse of 22 January 1843, recorded by William Clayton; *WJS*, 159.

man on earth unto whom God revealed his word and gave power and authority to administer in his name. And where there is a priest of God, a minister who has power and authority from God to administer in the ordinances of the gospel and officiate in the priesthood of God, there is the kingdom of God. . . .

Where did the kingdom of God begin? Where there is no kingdom of God there is no salvation. What constitutes the kingdom of God? Where there is a prophet, a priest, or a righteous man unto whom God gives his oracles, there is the kingdom of God. And where the oracles of God are not, there the kingdom of God is not. In these remarks I have no allusion to the kingdoms of the earth. . . . We speak of the kingdom of God on the earth, not the kingdom of men. . . .

John was a priest after his father and held the keys of the Aaronic Priesthood and was called of God to preach the gospel and the kingdom of God. The Jews as a nation having departed from the law of God and the gospel, the Lord prepared the way for transferring it to the Gentiles. "But," says one, "the kingdom of God could not be set up in the days of John, for John said the kingdom was at hand." But I would ask if it could be any nearer to them than to be in the hands of John. The people needed not wait for the days of Pentecost to find the kingdom of God, for John had it with him. He came forth from the wilderness crying out, "Repent ye: for the kingdom of heaven is at hand," as much as to bawl out: "Here, I have got the kingdom of God and I am coming after you. I've got the kingdom of God, and you can get it. I am coming after you, and if you don't receive it, you will be damned." The scriptures represent that all Jerusalem went out unto John's baptism. Here was a legal administrator, and those that were baptized were subjects for a King. Also, the laws and oracles of God were there; therefore the kingdom of God was there, for no man could have better authority to administer than John, and our Savior submitted to that authority himself by being baptized by John. Therefore, the kingdom of God was set up upon the earth, even in the days of John. . . .

It is evident the kingdom of God was on the earth, and John prepared subject[s] for [the] kingdom by preaching the gospel to them and baptizing them. He prepared the way before the Savior, or came as a forerunner and prepared subject[s] for the preaching of Christ. . . . Whenever men can find out the will of God and find an administrator legally authorized from God, there is the kingdom of God. But where these are not, the kingdom of God is not. All the ordinances, systems, and administrations on the earth are of no use to the children of men unless they are ordained and authorized of God, for nothing will save a man but a legal administrator. For none others will be acknowledged, either by God or angels.[5]

When the set time was come, John came forth. And when he took up his priesthood, he came bounding out of the wilderness, saying, "Repent ye: for the kingdom of heaven is at hand." He, having received the holy anointing, was the only lawful administrator, and the Jews all knew it. . . . All Jerusalem and all Judea came out to be baptized of John: Sadducees, Pharisees, Essenes.[6]

All the power, authority, and anointing descended upon the head of John the Baptist. . . . This was virtually acknowledged by all Judea and Jerusalem coming out to be baptized of him.[7]

The spirit of Elias was a going-before, to prepare the way for the greater, which was the case with John the Baptist. He came bawling through the wilderness: "Prepare ye the way of the Lord, and make his paths straight." They were informed if they could receive it, it was the spirit of Elias.[8]

See also under Mark 1:4; Luke 3:16; 16:16.

---

[5]Discourse of 22 January 1843, recorded by Wilford Woodruff; *WJS*, 156–58.

[6]Discourse of 23 July 1843, recorded by James Burgess; *WJS*, 235.

[7]Discourse of 23 July 1843, recorded by Franklin D. Richards; *WJS*, 236.

[8]Discourse of 10 March 1844, recorded by Wilford Woodruff; *WJS*, 327–28.

Matthew 3:8–10

From the moment John's voice was first heard, he was the pruner on the earth.[9]

Matthew 3:11

See under Luke 3:16.

Matthew 3:13–15

After John had been testifying of Jesus for some time, Jesus came unto him for baptism. John felt that the honor of baptizing his master was too great a thing—greater than he could claim—and said, "I have need to be baptized of thee, and comest thou to me?" Jesus replied: "Thus it behooveth us to fulfill all righteousness," thus signifying to John the claim of the Aaronic Priesthood, which holds the keys of entrance into the kingdom. . . . Jesus could not enter except by the administration of John.[10]

Jesus Christ himself . . . had no need of repentance, having done no sin. According to his solemn declaration to John: "Now let me be baptized" (for no man can enter the kingdom without obeying this ordinance), "for thus it becometh us to fulfil all righteousness." Surely, then, if it became John and Jesus Christ, the Savior, to fulfil all righteousness to be baptized, so surely, then, it will become every other person that seeks the kingdom of heaven to go and do likewise. For he is the door, and if any person climbs up any other way, the same is a thief and a robber [John 10:1].[11]

Christ fulfilled all righteousness in becoming obedient to the

---

[9]Discourse of 29 January 1843, recorded by Willard Richards; *WJS,* 162.

[10]Discourse of 21 March 1841, recorded by Martha Jane Coray; *WJS,* 66.

[11]*Times and Seasons,* 1 September 1842, 905.

law which [he] himself had given to Moses on the mount and thereby magnified it and made it honorable instead of destroying it.[12]

"John, I must be baptized by you. Why? To answer my decrees." John refuses. Jesus had no legal administrator before John. [There is] no salvation between the two lids of the Bible without a legal administrator.[13]

Men will set up stakes and say, "Thus far will we go, and no farther." . . . Did the Savior? No, [we] view him fulfilling all righteousness again on the banks of Jordan, . . . setting up no stake but coming right up to the mark in all things.[14]

Matthew 3:16

The dove which sat upon his shoulder was a sure testimony that he was of God.[15]

The Holy Ghost cannot be transformed into a dove, but the sign of a dove was given to John to signify the truth of the deed, as the dove was an emblem or token of truth.[16]

[The sign of the dove was] instituted before the creation. [The] Devil could not come in [the] sign of a dove. [The] Holy Ghost is a personage in the form of a personage. [He] does not confine [himself] to [the] form of a dove, but in [the] sign of a dove.[17]

---

[12]Discourse of 29 January 1843, recorded by Franklin D. Richards; *WJS*, 162–63.

[13]Discourse of 23 July 1843, recorded by Willard Richards; *WJS*, 235.

[14]Discourse of 27 August 1843, recorded by James Burgess; *WJS*, 246.

[15]Discourse of 21 March 1841, recorded by Martha Jane Coray; *WJS*, 66.

[16]Discourse of 29 January 1843, recorded by Franklin D. Richards; *WJS*, 163.

[17]Discourse of 29 January 1843, recorded by Willard Richards; *WJS*, 160.

Matthew 4:21

It tells about Jacobus. [It] means Jacob, in the English James. . . . Matthew 4:21 gives the testimony that it is Jacob. . . . Latin says that Iacobus means Jacob; Hebrew says [it] means Jacob; Greek says Jacob; German says Jacob.[18]

It tells about Jacobus the son of Zebedee. [It] means Jacob. The New Testament says James. Now if Jacob had the keys, you might talk about James through all eternity and never get the keys. Matthew 4:21 gives the word Jacob instead of James. . . . Read from the Hebrew: Yaʿaqōb, Jacob; Greek Iakōbos, Jacob; Latin Iacobus, Jacob too.[19]

Jacob the son of Zebedee, to form James the son of Zebedee, [as in] Greek, Hebrew, German, and Latin.[20]

Matthew 5:5

We rejoice that the time is at hand when the wicked who will not repent will be swept from the earth with the besom of destruction, and the earth become an inheritance for the poor and the meek.[21]

We rejoice in our hearts that the time is at hand when those who persist in wickedness will be swept from the earth with the besom of destruction, and the earth become an inheritance for the poor and the meek.[22]

See also under Revelation 21:4.

---

[18]Discourse of 7 April 1844, recorded by Thomas Bullock; *KFD*, 41.

[19]Discourse of 7 April 1844, recorded by William Clayton; *KFD*, 40. The phrase "through all eternity" is added from the Bullock report; *KFD*, 41.

[20]Discourse of 7 April 1844, recorded by Willard Richards; *KFD*, 40.

[21]Journal, 2 December 1835; *PJS*, 2:93.

[22]1834–36 History, 1 December 1835; *PJS*, 1:150.

Matthew 5:9

If the nation, a single state, community, or family ought to be grateful for anything, it is peace. Peace, lovely child of heaven. Peace, like light from the same great parent, gratifies, animates, and happifies the just and the unjust and is the very essence of happiness below and bliss above. He that does not strive with all his powers of body and mind, with all his influence at home and abroad, and to cause others to do so too, to seek peace and maintain it for his own benefit and convenience and for the honor of his state, nation, and country, has no claim on the clemency of man, nor should he be entitled to the friendship of woman or the protection of government. He is the canker worm to gnaw his own vitals and the vulture to prey upon his own body. And he is as to his own prospects and prosperity in life a *felo de se*[23] of his own pleasure. A community of such beings are not far from hell on earth and should be let alone as unfit for the smiles of the free or the praise of the brave. But the peacemaker, Oh give ear to him! For the words of his mouth, and his doctrine, drop like the rain and distil as the dew. They are like the gentle mist upon the herbs and as the moderate shower upon the grass [Deut. 32:2].[24]

Matthew 5:10–12

Know this, when men thus deal with you and speak all manner of evil of you falsely for the sake of Christ, that he is your friend.[25]

Shall a man be considered bad when men speak evil of him?

[23]*Felo de se:* "In law, one who commits felony by suicide, or deliberately destroys his own life"; Noah Webster, *An American Dictionary of the English Language* (New York: S. Converse, 1828), s.v. *"felo de se."*

[24]*Times and Seasons,* 15 March 1844, 473.

[25]Letter to W. W. Phelps, John Whitmer, Edward Partridge, Isaac Morley, John Corrill, and Sidney Gilbert, 18 August 1833; *PWJS,* 285.

No! If a man stands and opposes the world of sin, he may expect all things arrayed against him.[26]

And if they persecute you, so persecuted they the prophets and righteous men that were before you. For all this there is a reward in heaven.[27]

Matthew 5:29–30

Now the fact is, if any of the members of our body are disordered, the rest of our body will be affected with them, and then all is brought into bondage together.[28]

Matthew 5:42

Every person in this Church has a right to control his own property and is not required to do anything except by his own free voluntary act, that he may impart to the poor according to the requirement of the gospel.[29]

Matthew 5:43–45

While one portion of the human race is judging and condemning the other without mercy, the great Parent of the universe looks upon the whole of the human family with a fatherly care and paternal regard. He views them as his offspring, and

---

[26]Discourse of 31 August 1842, recorded by Eliza R. Snow; *WJS*, 131.

[27]Letter to all the Saints in Nauvoo, 1 September 1842; *PJS*, 2:457; D&C 127:4.

[28]Letter to Edward Partridge, W. W. Phelps, John Whitmer, Algernon Sidney Gilbert, John Corrill, Isaac Morley, and all the Saints whom it may concern, from Kirtland Mills, Ohio, 10 December 1833; *PWJS*, 309.

[29]Letter to the editor of the *Chester County* (Pennsylvania) *Register and Examiner,* 22 January 1840; *PWJS*, 458.

without any of those contracted feelings that influence the children of men causes "his sun to rise on the evil and the good, and sends his rain on the just and unjust."[30]

If we would secure and cultivate the love of others, we must love others, even our enemies as well as friends.[31]

Matthew 6:1–2, 5, 16

The praise of men, or the honor of this world, is of no benefit.[32]

Matthew 7:1

See under Job 4–37.

Matthew 7:15–20

The servants of God teach nothing but the principles of eternal life. By their works ye shall know them. A good man will speak good things and holy principles, and an evil man, evil things. I feel in the name of the Lord to rebuke all such bad principles, liars, and so forth. And I warn all of you to look out who you are going after. I exhort you to give heed to all the virtue and the teachings which I have given you.[33]

Matthew 7:21–23

That which the world calls righteousness I have not any regard for. To be righteous is to be just and merciful. If a man fails in kindness, justice, and mercy, he will be damned.[34]

---

[30]*Times and Seasons,* 15 April 1842, 759.

[31]Discourse of 9 July 1843, recorded by Willard Richards; *WJS,* 229.

[32]1834–36 History, 5 December 1834; *PJS,* 1:25.

[33]Discourse of 12 May 1844, recorded by Thomas Bullock; *WJS,* 369.

[34]Discourse of 21 May 1843, recorded by Martha Jane Coray; *WJS,* 206.

Matthew 8:28–34

The great principle of happiness consists in having a body. The Devil has no body, and herein is his punishment. He is pleased when he can obtain the tabernacle of [a] man, and when cast out by the Savior, he asked to go into the herd of swine, showing that he would prefer a swine's body to having none. All beings who have bodies have power over those who have not. The Devil has no power over us, only as we permit him; the moment we revolt at anything which comes from God, the Devil takes power.[35]

The Devil is without a tabernacle, and the Lord has set bounds to all spirits. Hence comes the saying: "Thou son of David, why art thou come to torment us before the time?" Jesus commanded him to come out of the man, and the Devil besought him that he might enter in a herd of swine nearby. For the Devil knew they were a covetous people, and if he could kill their hogs, they would drive Jesus out of their coasts, and he then would have tabernacle[s] enough. Jesus permitted him to enter into the swine.[36]

Wicked spirits have their bounds, limits, and laws by which they are governed or controlled and know their future destiny. Hence those that were in the maniac said to our Savior, "Art thou come to torment us before the time?"[37]

The greatness of his punishment is that he shall not have a tabernacle; this is his punishment. So the Devil thinks to thwart the decree of God by going up and down in the earth seeking whom he may destroy—any person that he can find that will

---

[35]Discourse of 5 January 1841, recorded by William Clayton; *WJS,* 60.

[36]Discourse of 28 March 1841, recorded by William P. McIntire; *WJS,* 68.

[37]*Times and Seasons,* 1 April 1842, 745.

yield to him. He will bind him and take possession of the body and reign there, glorying in it mightily, not thinking that he had got a stolen tabernacle. By and by, someone of authority will come along and cast him out and restore the tabernacle to his rightful owner. But the Devil steals a tabernacle because he has not one of his own, but if he steals one he is liable to be turned out of doors.[38]

When Lucifer was hurled from heaven, the decree was that he should not obtain a tabernacle, nor those that were with him, but go abroad upon the earth exposed to the anger of the elements, naked and bare. But ofttimes he lays hold upon men, binds up their spirits, enters their habitations, laughs at the decree of God, and rejoices in that he hath a house to dwell in. By and by, he is expelled by authority and goes abroad mourning, naked upon the earth like a man without a house, exposed to the tempest and the storm.[39]

The mortification of Satan consists in his not being permitted to take a body. He sometimes gets possession of a body, but when the proven authorities turn him out of doors, he finds it was not his but a stolen one.[40]

Matthew 9:10–13
See under Mark 2:15–17.

Matthew 10:1
How have we come at the priesthood in the last days? It came

---

[38]Discourse of 14 May 1843, recorded by Wilford Woodruff; *WJS,* 201.

[39]Discourse of 21 May 1843, recorded by Martha Jane Coray; *WJS,* 207.

[40]Discourse of 21 May 1843, recorded by Franklin D. Richards; *WJS,* 208.

down in regular succession. Peter, James, and John had it given to them, and they gave it up.[41]

The apostles in ancient times held the keys of this priesthood—of the mysteries of the kingdom of God—and consequently were enabled to unlock and unravel all things pertaining to the government of the Church, the welfare of society, the future destiny of men, and the agency, power, and influence of spirits. For they could control [the spirits] at pleasure, bid them depart in the name of Jesus, and detect their mischievous and mysterious operations when trying to palm themselves upon the Church in a religious garb and militate against the interest of the Church and the spread of truth.[42]

Matthew 10:2

See under Matthew 4:21.

Matthew 10:34–35

The time is soon coming when no man will have any peace but in Zion and her stakes. I saw men hunting the lives of their own sons, and brother murdering brother, women killing their own daughters, and daughters seeking the lives of their mothers. I saw armies arrayed against armies. I saw blood, desolations, fires, and so forth. The Son of Man has said that the mother shall be against the daughter, and the daughter against the mother. These things are at our doors.[43]

Matthew 10:39, JST

"He that seeks to save his life shall lose it; but he that loseth

---

[41]Discourse of summer of 1839, recorded in Willard Richards's "Pocket Companion"; *WJS,* 9.

[42]*Times and Seasons,* 1 April 1842, 745.

[43]Discourse of summer of 1839, recorded in Willard Richards's "Pocket Companion"; *WJS,* 11.

his life for my sake and the gospel's shall find it," saith Jesus Christ.[44]

Matthew 11:11

John was great in that he baptized Jesus.[45]

How was John the greatest prophet ever born of a woman? How is the least in the kingdom greater than he? Answer to the first—his greatness consisted in three things. First, his appointment to prepare the way before the Lord Jesus Christ. Second, his privilege to baptize him or induct him into his kingdom. Third, his being the only legal administrator in the affairs of the kingdom that was then on the earth. Consequently, the Jews had to obey his instruction or be damned by their own law. . . .

Answer to [the] second query: Christ was least in the kingdom in their estimation, or least entitled to their credulity as a prophet, but as in truth, greater than John.[46]

How is it John was considered one of the greatest of prophets? Three things:

First, he was trusted with a divine mission of preparing the way before the face of the Lord. [Who ever received such] trust, before or since? No man. Second, He was trusted, and it was required at his hands, to baptize the Son of Man. Who ever did that? Who had so great a privilege and glory [to lead the] Son of God into the waters of baptism, beholding the Holy Ghost in the sign of a dove? . . . Third, John at that time was the only legal

---

[44]Letter to the Church in Caldwell County, from Liberty Jail, Missouri, 16 December 1838; *PWJS*, 382.

[45]Discourse of 21 March 1841, reported by Martha Jane Coray; *WJS*, 66.

[46]Discourse of 29 January 1843, recorded by Franklin D. Richards; *WJS*, 162–63.

administrator, holding the keys of power, there was on earth. The keys, the kingdom, the power, and the glory [had gone] from the Jews [to the] son of Zacharias, by the holy anointing [and] decree of heaven. These three constituted him the greatest born of woman.

[How is it that] he that is least in the kingdom is greater than he? Who did Jesus have reference to? Jesus was looked upon as having the least claim in all God's kingdom. "He that is considered the least among you is greater than John, that is, myself."[47]

Matthew 11:12

Now I will translate a little: The kingdom of heaven hath power and authority, and by that they take or enter legally and lawfully the kingdom of heaven.[48]

The rendering [of] the texts is: The kingdom continueth in authority or law, and the authority or legality (which belonged to John) took it by force, or wrested it from the Jews to be delivered to a nation bringing forth the fruits thereof.[49]

The kingdom of heaven suffereth violence, and the kingdom of heaven continueth in authority until John. The authority taketh it by absolute power. John, having the power, takes the kingdom by authority.[50]

Matthew 11:13–15

The Spirit of Elias is a forerunner, same as John the Baptist.[51]

Jesus said of John: "This is Elias, which was to come, if you

---

[47]Discourse of 29 January 1843, recorded by Willard Richards; *WJS,* 160.

[48]Discourse of 23 July 1843, recorded by James Burgess; *WJS,* 235.

[49]Discourse of 23 July 1843, recorded by Franklin D. Richards; *WJS,* 236.

[50]Discourse of 23 July 1843, recorded by Willard Richards; *WJS,* 234.

[51]Discourse of 10 March 1844, recorded by Thomas Bullock; *WJS,* 336.

will receive me. Otherwise he cannot do the work of an Elias. For Elias is preparatory for something greater, to prepare my way before me. I have power to restore all things and establish my kingdom amongst you, but if you will not receive me and my doctrine, he is not that Elias which was to come. For he cannot accomplish that for which he was sent."[52]

The spirit of Elias is to prepare the way for a greater revelation of God. [This] is the priesthood of Elias, or the priesthood that Aaron was ordained unto. And when God sends a man into the world to prepare for a greater work, [he] holds the keys of the power of Elias. It was called the doctrine of Elias even from the early ages of the world.[53]

See also under Matthew 3:1–6.

Matthew 12:31–32

All are within the reach of pardoning mercy who have not committed the unpardonable sin, which hath no forgiveness, neither in this world nor in the world to come.[54]

I have a declaration to make as to the provision which God made from before the foundation of the world. What has Jesus said? [For] all sins and all blasphemies—every transgression that man may be guilty of—there is a salvation for him [here] or in the world to come. Every spirit in the eternal world can be ferreted out and saved unless he has committed that sin which cannot be remitted to him. God has wrought out salvation for all men unless they have committed a certain sin. A friend who has got a friend in the world can save him unless he has committed

---

[52]Discourse of 10 March 1844, recorded by James Burgess; *WJS,* 333.

[53]Discourse of 10 March 1844, recorded by Wilford Woodruff; *WJS,* 328.

[54]Discourse of 3 October 1841, reported in *Times and Seasons,* 15 October 1841, 577.

the unpardonable sin. . . . He has got to say that the sun does not shine while he sees it. He has got to deny Jesus Christ when the heavens are open to him. . . . I warn you against all evil characters who sin against [the] Holy Ghost, for there is no redemption for them in this world nor in the world to come. . . . Those who sin against the Holy Ghost cannot be forgiven in this world or in the world to come. But they shall die the second death. As they concoct scenes of bloodshed in this world, so they shall rise to that resurrection which is as the lake of fire and brimstone.[55]

[I] speak in relation to the provisions God hath made to suit the conditions of man. What hath Jesus said? [For] all sins and blasphemies—every transgression except one—there is a provision either in this world or in the world of spirits. Hence God hath made a provision that every spirit can be ferreted out in that world that has not sinned the unpardonable sin. . . . After a man has sinned the sin against the Holy Spirit, there is no repentance for him.[56]

God made provisions before the world was for every creature in [it]. All sin shall be forgiven in this world or [the] world to come, except one. [There is] salvation for all men who have not committed the certain sin. . . . [One has] got to deny the plan of salvation, and so forth, with his eyes open. . . . Those who commit the unpardonable sin are damned to *'ôlām*, without end.[57]

All sins and blasphemy are to be forgiven except the sin against the Holy Ghost. . . . Any man that has a friend in eternity can save him if he has not committed the unpardonable sin. He cannot be damned through all eternity. . . . Jesus Christ will save

----

[55]Discourse of 7 April 1844, recorded by Thomas Bullock; *KFD,* 59, 67, 69, 81.

[56]Discourse of 7 April 1844, recorded by William Clayton; *KFD,* 58, 66.

[57]Discourse of 7 April 1844, recorded by Willard Richards; *KFD,* 58, 66, 80. The Hebrew word *'ôlām* means "eternity."

all except the sons of perdition. What must a man do to commit the unpardonable sin? They must receive the Holy Ghost, have the heavens opened unto them, and know God, and then sin against him. . . . There have also been remarks made concerning all men being redeemed from hell. But I say that any man who commits the unpardonable sin must dwell in hell worlds without end.[58]

See also under 2 Peter 1:10–11.

Matthew 12:33–35
See under Luke 6:43–45.

Matthew 13:1–3
I shall now proceed to make some remarks from the sayings of the Savior, recorded in the 13th chapter of his gospel according to St. Matthew, which in my mind afford us as clear an understanding upon the important subject of the gathering as anything recorded in the Bible.[59]

Matthew 13:3–9
This parable was spoken to demonstrate the effects that are produced by the preaching of the word. And we believe that it has an allusion directly to the commencement, or the setting up, of the kingdom in that age.[60]

Matthew 13:10–16
"And the disciples came, and said unto him, Why speakest

---

[58]Discourse of 7 April 1844, recorded by Wilford Woodruff; *KFD,* 58, 66, 80.

[59]*Messenger and Advocate,* December 1835, 225.

[60]*Messenger and Advocate,* December 1835, 226.

thou unto them in parables?" I would remark here that the "them" made use of in this interrogation is a personal pronoun and refers to the multitude. "He answered and said unto them," that is, the disciples, "it is given unto you to know the mysteries of the kingdom of heaven, but unto them," that is, unbelievers, "it is not given. For whosoever hath, to him shall be given, and he shall have more abundance: but whosoever hath not, from him shall be taken away even that he hath."

We understand from this saying that those who had been previously looking for a Messiah to come, according to the testimony of the prophets, and were then at that time looking for a Messiah but had not sufficient light, on account of their unbelief, to discern him to be their Savior—and he being the true Messiah—consequently, they must be disappointed and lose even all the knowledge, or have taken away from them, all the light, understanding, and faith which they had upon this subject. Therefore, he that will not receive the greater light must have taken away from him all the light which he hath. And "if the light which is in you become darkness, behold, how great is that darkness!" [Matt. 6:23]. . . . Now we discover that the very reason assigned by [Isaiah] why they would not receive the Messiah was because they did not or would not understand [Isa. 6:9–10]. And seeing, they did not perceive. . . .

We draw the conclusion, then, that the very reason why the multitude, or the world, as they were designated by the Savior, did not receive an explanation upon his parables was because of unbelief. "To you," he says speaking to his disciples, "it is given to know the mysteries of the kingdom of God." And why? Because of the faith and confidence they had in him.[61]

Matthew 13:16

We find that the very principle upon which the disciples were accounted blessed was because they were permitted to see with

---

[61]*Messenger and Advocate,* December 1835, 225–26.

their eyes and hear with their ears. And the condemnation which rested upon the multitude, which received not his saying, was because they were not willing to see with their eyes and hear with their ears—not because they *could* not and were not privileged to see and hear, but because their hearts were full of iniquity and abomination: "As your fathers did so do ye." The prophet, foreseeing that they would thus harden their hearts, plainly declared it [Isa. 6:9–10]. And herein is the condemnation of the world: "that light hath come into the world, and men choose darkness rather than light, because their deeds are evil" [John 3:19]. This is so plainly taught by the Savior that a wayfaring man need not mistake it.[62]

Matthew 13:18–19

Men are in the habit, when the truth is exhibited by the servants of God, of saying, "All is mystery; they have spoken in parables and therefore are not to be understood." It is true they have eyes to see and see not. But none are so blind as those who will not see. And although the Savior spoke this parable to such characters, yet unto his disciples he expounded it plainly. And we have reason to be truly humble before the God of our fathers that he hath left these things on record for us, so plain that notwithstanding the exertions and combined influence of the priests of Baal, they have not power to blind our eyes and darken our understanding, if we will but open our eyes and read with candor, for a moment.

But listen to the explanation of the parable: "When any one heareth the word of the kingdom, and understandeth it not, then cometh the wicked one, and catcheth away that which was sown in his heart." Now mark the expression, "that which was before sown in his heart." "This is he which received seed by the way

---

[62]*Messenger and Advocate,* December 1835, 225–26.

side." Men who have no principle of righteousness in themselves, and whose hearts are full of iniquity, and who have no desire for the principles of truth, do not understand the word of truth when they hear it. The devil taketh away the word of truth out of their hearts, because there is no desire for righteousness in them.[63]

Matthew 13:22

"He also that received seed among the thorns is he that receiveth the word; and the cares of this world, and the deceitfulness of riches, choke the word, and he becometh unfruitful."[64]

Matthew 13:24–30, 36–43

Now we learn by this parable not only the setting up of the kingdom in the days of the Savior, which is represented by the good seed which produced fruit, but also the corruptions of the Church, which are represented by the tares which were sown by the enemy, which his disciples would fain have plucked up, or cleansed the Church of, if their views had been favored by the Savior. But he, knowing all things, says, "Not so," as much as to say, "Your views are not correct; the Church is in its infancy, and if you take this rash step, you will destroy the wheat, or the Church, with the tares. Therefore, it is better to let them grow together until the harvest, or the end of the world, which means the destruction of the wicked, which is not yet fulfilled." . . .

Now men cannot have any possible grounds to say that this is figurative, or that it does not mean what it says, for he is now explaining what he had previously spoken in parables. And according to this language, the end of the world is the destruction of the wicked. The harvest and the end of the world have an allusion directly to the human family in the last days—instead of the

---

[63]*Messenger and Advocate,* December 1835, 226.

[64]*Messenger and Advocate,* December 1835, 226.

earth as many have imagined—and that which shall precede the coming of the Son of Man and the restitution of all things spoken of by the mouth of all the holy prophets since the world began. And the angels are to have something to do in this great work, for they are the reapers.

As therefore the tares are gathered and burned in the fire, so shall it be in the end of this world. That is, as the servants of God go forth warning the nations, both priests and people, and as they harden their hearts and reject the light of the truth, these first being delivered over to the buffetings of Satan, and the law and the testimony being closed up as it was with the Jews, they are left in darkness and delivered over unto the day of burning. Thus, being bound up by their creeds and their bands made strong by their priests, [they] are prepared for the fulfillment of the saying of the Savior: "The Son of man shall send forth his angels and gather out of his kingdom all things that offend, and them which do iniquity; and shall cast them into a furnace of fire, and there shall be wailing and gnashing of teeth."

We understand that the work of the gathering together of the wheat into barns, or garners, is to take place while the tares are being bound over and preparing for the day of burning, that after the day of burnings, "the righteous shall shine forth like the sun in the kingdom of their Father. Who hath ears to hear, let him hear."[65]

God sows. The enemy comes and sows parties, divisions, and heresies. "Shall we kill them?" "No, not till harvest, the end of the world." The Son of God will do as he ever has done from the beginning: send forth his angels. If the reapers do not come, the wheat cannot be saved. Nothing but [the] kingdom being restored can save the world.[66]

---

[65]*Messenger and Advocate,* December 1835, 226–29.

[66]Discourse of summer of 1839, recorded in Willard Richards's "Pocket Companion"; *WJS,* 13.

Matthew 13:31–32

And again, "another parable put he forth unto them," having an allusion to the kingdom which should be set up just previous [to], or at the time of, the harvest. Now we can discover plainly that this figure is given to represent the Church as it shall come forth in the last days. Behold, the kingdom of heaven is likened unto it. Now, what is like unto it?

Let us take the Book of Mormon, which a man took and hid in his field, securing it by his faith to spring up in the last days, or in due time. Let us behold it coming forth out of the ground which is indeed accounted the least of all seeds. But behold it branching forth, yea, even towering with lofty branches and God-like majesty, until it becomes the greatest of all herbs. And it is truth, and it has sprouted and come forth out of the earth, and righteousness begins to look down from heaven, and God is sending down his powers, gifts, and angels to lodge in the branches thereof.

The kingdom of heaven is like unto a mustard seed. Behold, then, is not this the kingdom of heaven that is raising its head in the last days in the majesty of its God, even the Church of the Latter-day Saints?—like an impenetrable, immovable rock in the midst of the mighty deep, exposed to the storms and tempests of Satan but [which] has, thus far, remained steadfast and is still braving the mountain waves of opposition which are driven by the tempestuous winds of sinking crafts [and] have [been] and are still dashing with tremendous foam across its triumphing brow, urged onward with redoubled fury by the enemy of righteousness with his pitchfork of lies. . . .

[A] cloud of darkness has long been beating with mountain waves upon the immovable rock of the Church of the Latter-day Saints. And notwithstanding all this, the mustard seed is still towering its lofty branches, higher and higher, and extending itself wider and wider. And the chariot wheels of the kingdom are still rolling on, impelled by the mighty arm of Jehovah, and in spite of all opposition will still roll on until his words are all fulfilled.[67]

The mustard seed is small but brings forth a large tree, and the fowls lodge in the branches. The fowls are the angels. . . . These angels come down, combined together to gather their children, and gather them.[68]

Matthew 13:33

It may be understood that the Church of the Latter-day Saints has taken its rise from a little leaven that was put into three witnesses. Behold how much this is like the parable: it is fast leavening the lump and will soon leaven the whole. . . .

Three measures of meal, undergoing the purifying touch by a revelation of Jesus Christ and the ministering of angels, who have already commenced this work in the last days which will answer to the leaven which leavened the whole lump.[69]

It alludes expressly to the last days, when there should be little faith on the earth and it [will] leaven the whole world. There shall be safety in Zion and Jerusalem and [among] the remnants whom the Lord shall call. It refers to the priesthood.[70]

Matthew 13:36–43

See under Matthew 13:24–30, 36–43.

---

[67]*Messenger and Advocate,* December 1835, 227–28.

[68]Discourse of summer of 1839, recorded in Willard Richards's "Pocket Companion"; *WJS,* 10.

[69]*Messenger and Advocate,* December 1835, 228–29.

[70]Statement of 22 December 1842, recorded by Willard Richards; *PJS,* 3.

Matthew 13:40

What is the end of the world? The destruction of the wicked.[71]

Matthew 13:44

For the work after this pattern, see the Church of the Latter-day Saints, selling all that they have and gathering themselves together unto a place that they may purchase for an inheritance, that they may be together and bear each other's afflictions in the day of calamity.[72]

This figure is a representation of the [kingdom] in the last days.[73]

Matthew 13:45–46

For the work of this example, see men traveling to find places for Zion and her stakes or remnants, who, when they find the place for Zion, or the pearl of great price, straightway sell that they have and buy it.[74]

The pearl of great price is the inheritance prepared for the Saints.[75]

Matthew 13:47–50

For the work of this pattern, behold the seed of Joseph

---

[71]Discourse of summer of 1839, recorded in Willard Richards's "Pocket Companion"; *WJS*, 13.

[72]*Messenger and Advocate*, December 1835, 229.

[73]Discourse of summer of 1839, recorded in Willard Richards's "Pocket Companion"; *WJS*, 13.

[74]*Messenger and Advocate*, December 1835, 229.

[75]Discourse of summer of 1839, recorded in Willard Richards's "Pocket Companion"; *WJS*, 13.

spreading forth the gospel net upon the face of the earth, gathering of every kind, that the good may be saved in vessels prepared for that purpose, and the angels will take care of the bad.[76]

Matthew 13:51

And we say, "Yea, Lord." And well might they say, "Yea, Lord," for these things are so plain and so glorious that every Saint in that last days must respond with a hearty "Amen" to them.[77]

Matthew 13:52

For the work of this example, see the Book of Mormon coming forth out of the treasure of the heart, also the covenants given to the Latter-day Saints, also the translation of the Bible, thus bringing forth out of the heart things new and old.[78]

Matthew 16:18

Jesus in his teaching says: "Upon this rock I will build my church; and the gates of hell shall not prevail against it." What rock? Revelation.[79]

Matthew 16:19

Or, in other words, taking a different view of the translation, whatsoever you record on earth shall be recorded in heaven, and whatsoever you do not record on earth shall not be recorded in heaven. . . . It may seem to some to be a very bold doctrine that we talk of—a power which records or binds on earth and binds in heaven. Nevertheless, in all ages of the world, whenever the

---

[76]*Messenger and Advocate,* December 1835, 229.

[77]*Messenger and Advocate,* December 1835, 229.

[78]*Messenger and Advocate,* December 1835, 229.

[79]Discourse of 22 January 1843, recorded by Wilford Woodruff; *WJS,* 158.

Lord has given a dispensation of the priesthood to any man by actual revelation, or any set of men, this power has always been given. Hence, whatsoever those men did in authority, in the name of the Lord, and did it truly and faithfully, and kept a proper and faithful record of the same, it became a law on earth and in heaven, and could not be annulled, according to the decrees of the great Jehovah. . . .

Now the great and grand secret of the whole matter, and the *summum bonum* of the whole subject that is lying before us, consists in obtaining the powers of the Holy Priesthood. For him to whom these keys are given there is no difficulty in obtaining a knowledge of facts in relation to the salvation of the children of men, both as well for the dead as for the living. . . . This, therefore, is the sealing and binding power, and, in one sense of the word, the keys of the kingdom, which consist in the key of knowledge.[80]

Matthew 16:25–26

A good man will endure all things to honor Christ and dispose of the whole world and all in it to save his soul.[81]

See also under Matthew 10:39, JST.

Matthew 17:1–8

The priesthood is everlasting. The Savior, Moses, and Elias gave the keys to Peter, James, and John on the mount, when they were transfigured before him.[82]

Men will set up stakes and say, "Thus far will we go, and no

---

[80]*Times and Seasons,* 1 October 1842, 934–35; D&C 128:8–9, 11, 14.

[81]Letter to Abijah Tewksbury, from Nauvoo, Illinois, 4 June 1844; *PWJS,* 581.

[82]Discourse of summer of 1839, recorded in Willard Richards's "Pocket Companion"; *WJS,* 9.

farther." . . . Did the Savior? No, [we] view him . . . on the mount transfigured before Peter and John, there receiving the fulness of priesthood, or the law of God, setting up no stake but coming right up to the mark in all things.[83]

Matthew 17:10–13

See under Matthew 11:13–15.

Matthew 18:18

See under Matthew 16:19.

Matthew 19:28

In the day of judgment, [God] designs to make us the judges of the generation in which we live.[84]

Matthew 20:25–28

The true principle of honor in the Church of the Saints, that the more a man is exalted the more humble he will be—if actuated by the Spirit of the Lord—seem[s] to have been overlooked. And the fact that the greatest is least and servant of all, as said our Savior, [seems] never to have been thought of.[85]

Matthew 22:1–14

In the 22nd chapter of Matthew's[86] account of the Messiah, we find the kingdom of heaven likened unto a king who made a marriage for his son. That this son was the Messiah will not be

---

[83]Discourse of 27 August 1843, recorded by James Burgess; *WJS,* 246.

[84]Letter to W. W. Phelps, John Whitmer, Edward Partridge, Isaac Morley, John Corrill, and Sidney Gilbert, 18 August 1833; *PWJS,* 287.

[85]1834–36 History, 5 December 1834; *PJS,* 1:23.

[86]The original publication incorrectly cites Luke 22 here.

disputed, since it was the kingdom of heaven that was represented in the parable. And that the Saints, or those who are found faithful to the Lord, are the individuals who will be found worthy to inherit a seat at the marriage supper is evident from the sayings of John in Revelation: " . . . The marriage of the Lamb is come, and his wife hath made herself ready. And to her was granted that she should be arrayed in fine linen, clean and white: for the fine linen is the righteousness of saints" [Rev. 19:7–8].[87]

Matthew 22:14

There has been a great difficulty in getting anything into the heads of this generation. . . . Even the Saints are slow to understand. I have tried for a number of years to get the minds of the Saints prepared to receive the things of God, but we frequently see [that] some of them, after suffering all they have for the work of God, will fly to pieces like glass as soon as anything comes that is contrary to their traditions. They cannot stand the fire at all. How many will be able to abide a celestial law and go through and receive their exaltation? I am unable to say, but many are called, and few are chosen.[88]

Matthew 22:23–30

See under Luke 20:27–36.

Matthew 23:13–33

So soon as [the Israelites] began to be puffed up with self-sufficiency, they too, like the ancients, honored the *old* revelations in word, or profession, but they stoned the prophets which came with *new* ones—not because God had ever said that he had ceased to give line upon line, precept upon precept, here

---

[87]*Evening and Morning Star,* March 1834, 144.

[88]Discourse of 21 January 1844, recorded by Wilford Woodruff; *WJS,* 319.

a little and there a little, but because they chose darkness rather than light because their deeds were evil.

The same principle was signally manifest among the Jews when the Savior came in the flesh. These then-religious bigots boasted of the old revelations, garnished the sepulchers of the dead, gave tithes of mint and anise, made long prayers for a pretense, and crossed sea and land to make proselytes. But yet when the new revelation came fresh from the mouth of the great I AM himself, they could not endure it. It was too much. It showed the corruptions of that generation, as others before.[89]

Matthew 23:34–36

As they possessed greater privileges than any other generation, not only pertaining to themselves but to their dead, their sin was greater, as they not only neglected their own salvation but that of their progenitors. And hence their blood was required at their hands.[90]

Matthew 23:37–38

The reason why the Jews were scattered and their house left unto them desolate was because they refused to be gathered, that the fulness of the priesthood might be revealed among them, which never can be done but by the gathering of the people.[91]

Whence are [they] in the curse of Almighty God that was to be poured out upon the heads of the Jews? [Because] they would not be gathered, because they would not let Christ gather them. It was the design in the councils of heaven before the world was that the principle and law of [the] priesthood was predicated upon the gathering of the people in every age of the world. Jesus

---

[89]*Times and Seasons,* 15 August 1842, 890.

[90]*Times and Seasons,* 15 April 1842, 761.

[91]Discourse of 11 June 1843, recorded by Franklin D. Richards; *WJS,* 215.

did everything possible to gather the people. They would not be gathered, and he poured out curses upon them.[92]

What was the object of gathering the Jews together, or the people of God in any age of the world? The main object was to build unto the Lord a house, whereby he could reveal unto his people the ordinances of his house and glories of his kingdom, and teach the people the ways of salvation. For there are certain ordinances and principles that when they are taught and practiced must be done in a place or house built for that purpose. This was purposed in the mind of God before the world was, and it was for this purpose that God designed to gather together the Jews oft. But they would not. It is for the same purpose that God gathers together the people in the last days, to build unto the Lord a house to prepare them for the ordinances, endowment, washings, and anointings. . . . It was one reason why Jesus said, "How oft would I have gathered you (the Jews) together," that they might attend to the ordinance of the baptism for the dead, as well as the other ordinances, the priesthood, revelations, and so forth. This was the case on the day of Pentecost. These blessings were poured out upon the disciples on that occasion. . . .

Why gather the people together in this place? For the same purpose that Jesus wanted to gather the Jews: to receive the ordinances, the blessings, and the glories that God has in store for his Saints.[93]

Matthew 24:3 (Joseph Smith–Matthew 1:4)

See under Matthew 13:40.

Matthew 24:6–7, 12–13 (Joseph Smith–Matthew 1:28–30)

There will be here and there a stake for the gathering of the

---

[92]Discourse of 11 June 1843, recorded by Willard Richards; *WJS,* 210.

[93]Discourse of 11 June 1843, recorded by Wilford Woodruff; *WJS,* 212–13, 214.

Saints. Some may have cried "Peace!" but the Saints and the world will have little peace from henceforth. Let this not hinder us from going to the stakes, for God has told us to flee, not dallying, or we shall be scattered, one here, another there. There your children shall be blessed, and you [shall be] in the midst of friends where you may be blessed. The gospel net gathers of every kind. I prophesy that the man who tarries after he has an opportunity of going will be afflicted by the Devil. Wars are at hand; we must not delay. . . .

We ought to have the building up of Zion as our greatest object. When wars come we shall have to flee to Zion. The cry is to make haste. The last revelation says, "Ye shall not have time to have gone over the earth until these things come" [cf. Matt. 10:23]. It will come as did the cholera—war, fires burning, earthquake, one pestilence after another.[94]

It is a false idea that the Saints will escape all the judgments while the wicked suffer, for all flesh is subject to suffer, and the righteous shall hardly escape. Still, many of the Saints will escape, for the just shall live by faith. Yet many of the righteous shall fall prey to disease, to pestilence, and so forth, by reason of the weakness of the flesh, and yet be saved in the kingdom of God.[95]

I prophesy in the name of the Lord God that the commencement of bloodshed as preparatory to the coming of the Son of Man will commence in South Carolina. (It probably may come through the slave trade.) This the voice declared to me while I was praying earnestly on the subject [on] 25 December 1832.[96]

See also under Matthew 24:27–30.

---

[94]Discourse of summer of 1839, recorded in Willard Richards's "Pocket Companion"; *WJS*, 11.

[95]Discourse of 29 September 1839, recorded by James Mulholland; *PJS*, 2:332.

[96]Discourse of 2 April 1843, recorded by Willard Richards; *WJS*, 172; see D&C 130:12–13.

Matthew 24:14a (Joseph Smith–Matthew 1:31)

The servants of God will not have gone over the nations of the Gentiles with a warning voice until the destroying angel will commence to waste the inhabitants of the earth. And as the prophet hath said, "it shall be a vexation to hear the report" [Isa. 28:19]. I speak because I feel for my fellow men; I do it in the name of the Lord, being moved upon by the Holy Spirit. Oh that I could snatch them from the vortex of misery into which I behold them plunging themselves by their sins, that I may be enabled, by the warning voice, to be an instrument of bringing them to unfeigned repentance, that they might have faith to stand in the evil day.[97]

When you are endowed and prepared to preach the gospel to all nations, kindreds, and tongues in their own languages, you must faithfully warn all, bind up the law, and seal up the testimony. And the destroying angel will follow close at your heels and execute his tremendous mission upon the children of disobedience and destroy the workers of iniquity, while the Saints will be gathered out from among them and stand in holy places ready to meet the Bridegroom when he comes.[98]

Matthew 24:14b (Joseph Smith–Matthew 1:31)

When [this verse] is rightly understood, it will be edifying. . . . The Savior said, when those tribulations should take place, it should be committed to a man who should be a witness over the whole world. The keys of knowledge, power, and revelations should be revealed to a witness who should hold the testimony to the world. It has always been my province to dig up hidden mysteries, new things, for my hearers. Just at the time when some men think that I have no right to the keys of the priesthood, just

---

[97]*Messenger and Advocate,* November 1835, 211.

[98]1834–36 History, discourse of 12 November 1835; *PJS,* 1:135; cf. *PJS,* 2:77–78.

at that time I have the greatest right. . . . All the testimony is that the Lord in the last days would commit the keys of the priesthood to a witness over all people. Has the gospel of the kingdom commenced in the last days? And will God take it from the man until he takes him himself? I have read it precisely as the words flowed from the lips of Jesus Christ. . . . John saw the angel having the holy priesthood who should preach the everlasting gospel to all nations [Rev. 14:6]. God had an angel, a special messenger, ordained and prepared for that purpose in the last days. Wo! Wo! be to that man, or set of men, who lift up their hands against God and his witness in these last days. For they shall deceive almost the very chosen ones. . . . Every man who has a calling to minister to the inhabitants of the world was ordained to that very purpose in the Grand Council of Heaven before this world was. I suppose that I was ordained to this very office in that Grand Council. . . . God will always protect me until my mission is fulfilled.[99]

The original translation reads thus: "And I will send you another witness, and he shall preach this gospel to all nations, to the ends of the world." But wo to that man or woman who shall lift up their or his hands against God's witness, for they are raising their hands or arms against the power of God, and they will be cursed.[100]

"Preached to a man who should be a witness to all people," is the meaning of the text.[101]

Matthew 24:24 (Joseph Smith–Matthew 1:22)

Until we have perfect love, we are liable to fall. And when we have a testimony that our names are sealed in the Lamb's

---

[99]Discourse of 12 May 1844, recorded by Thomas Bullock; *WJS,* 366–67.

[100]Discourse of 12 May 1844, recorded by George Laub; *WJS,* 369–70.

[101]Discourse of 12 May 1844, recorded by Samuel W. Richards; *WJS,* 371.

book of life, we have perfect love, and then it is impossible for false Christs to deceive us.[102]

When a man goes about prophesying and commands men to obey his teachings, he must be either a true or false prophet. False prophets always arise to oppose the true prophets, and they will prophesy so very near the truth that they will deceive almost the very chosen ones.[103]

But in these times in the last days, there will many false prophets arise, and false teachers, and deceive many. They shall have many followers by their deceit. They strive to have power and by their pernicious ways lead off many.[104]

Matthew 24:27–30 (Joseph Smith–Matthew 1:26, 33, 36)

We see that perilous times have come, as was testified of. We may look then with most perfect assurance for the rolling in of all those things that have been written. And with more confidence than ever before, [we] lift up our eyes to the luminary of day and say in our hearts, "Soon thou wilt veil thy blushing face." He that said, "Let there be light"—and there was light—hath spoken this word. And again, "Thou moon, thou dimmer light, thou luminary of night, shalt turn to blood." We see that everything is fulfilling, and the time shall soon come when the Son of Man shall descend in the clouds of heaven.[105]

I will prophesy that the signs of the coming of the Son of Man are already commenced. One pestilence will desolate after

---

[102]Statement of 25 October 1831; *Far West Record: Minutes of The Church of Jesus Christ of Latter-day Saints, 1830–1844*, ed. Donald Q. Cannon and Lyndon W. Cook (Salt Lake City: Deseret Book, 1983), 23.

[103]Discourse of 12 May 1844, recorded by Thomas Bullock; *WJS,* 367.

[104]Discourse of 12 May 1844, recorded by George Laub; *WJS,* 370.

[105]Letter to the Church at Quincy, Illinois, from Liberty Jail, Missouri, 20 March 1839; *PWJS,* 392.

another. We shall soon have war and bloodshed. The moon will be turned to blood. I testify of these things and that the coming of the Son of Man is nigh, even at your doors. If our souls and our bodies are not looking forth for the coming of the Son of Man, and after we are dead if we are not looking forth, we shall be among those who are calling for the rocks to fall upon us.[106]

We realize that perilous times have come, as have been testified of in ancient days, and we may look with certainty and the most perfect assurance for the rolling in of all those things which have been spoken of by all the holy prophets. Lift up your eyes to the bright luminary of day, and you can say, "Soon thou shalt veil thy blushing face, for at the behest of him who said 'Let there be light'—and there was light—thou shalt withdraw thy shining." "Thou moon, thou dimmer light and luminary of night, shalt turn to blood." We see that the prophecies concerning the last days are fulfilling, and the time shall soon come when the Son of Man shall descend in the clouds of heaven, in power and great glory.[107]

[A certain man][108] has not seen the sign of the Son of Man as foretold by Jesus. Neither has any man, nor will any man, till after the sun shall have been darkened and the moon bathed in blood. For the Lord hath not shown *me* any such sign, and as the prophet saith, so it must be: "Surely the Lord God will do nothing, but he revealeth his secret unto his servants the prophets" [Amos 3:7]. Therefore, hear this, O earth: the Lord will not come to reign over the righteous in this world in 1843, nor until everything for the Bridegroom is ready.[109]

---

[106]Discourse of summer of 1839, recorded in Willard Richards's "Pocket Companion"; *WJS,* 10–11.

[107]*Times and Seasons,* May 1840, 100.

[108]A man named Hiram Redding claimed to have seen the sign of Christ's coming.

[109]*Times and Seasons,* 1 March 1843, 113.

How are we to see it? As the lighting up of the morning or the dawning of the morning cometh from the east and shineth unto the west, so also is the coming of the Son of Man. The dawning of the morning makes its appearance in the east and moves along gradually. So also will the coming of the Son of Man be. It will be small at its first appearance and gradually become larger until every eye shall see it. Shall the Saints understand it? Oh yes. Paul says so [1 Thes. 5:4–5]. Shall the wicked understand? Oh no. They [will] attribute it to a natural cause. They will probably suppose it is two great comets coming in contact with each other. It will be small at first and will grow larger and larger until it will be all in a blaze, so that every eye shall see it.[110]

The coming of the Son of Man never will be, never can be, till the judgments spoken of for this hour are poured out, which judgments are commenced. . . . All this must be done before [the] Son of Man will make his appearance: wars and rumors of wars, signs in the heavens above [and] on the earth beneath, [the] sun turned into darkness [and the] moon to blood, earthquakes in diverse places, oceans heaving beyond their bounds, then one grand sign of the Son of Man in heaven. But what will the world do? They will say it is a planet, a comet, and so forth. Consequently, the Son of Man will come as the sign of [the] coming of the Son of Man.[111]

Matthew 24:32–33 (Joseph Smith–Matthew 1:38–39)

When you see the fig tree begin to put forth its leaves, you may know that the summer is nigh at hand. There will be a short work on the earth; it has now commenced. I suppose there will soon be perplexity all over the earth. Do not let our hearts faint when these things come upon us, for they must come or the word cannot be fulfilled. I know that something will soon take place to

---

[110]Discourse of 6 April 1843, recorded by James Burgess; *WJS*, 181.

[111]Discourse of 6 April 1843, recorded by Willard Richards; *WJS*, 180.

stir up this generation to see what they have been doing, and that their fathers have inherited lies, and they have been led captive by the Devil to no profit. But they know not what they do.[112]

Matthew 24:36 (Joseph Smith–Matthew 1:40)

I was once praying very earnestly to know the time of the coming of the Son of Man, when I heard a voice repeat the following: "Joseph, my son, if thou livest until thou art eighty-five years old, thou shalt see the face of the Son of Man. Therefore, let this suffice, and trouble me no more on this matter." I was left thus without being able to decide whether this coming referred to the beginning of the Millennium or to some previous appearing, or whether I should die and thus see his face. I believe the coming of the Son of Man will not be any sooner than that time.[113]

I earnestly desired to know concerning the coming of the Son of Man and prayed, when a voice said to me, "Joseph, my son, if thou livest until thou art eighty-five years old, thou shalt see the face of the Son of Man. Therefore, let this suffice and trouble me no more on this matter."[114]

I was once praying earnestly upon this subject, and a voice said unto me, "My son, if thou livest till thou art eighty-five years of age, thou shalt see the face of the Son of Man." I was left to draw my own conclusions concerning this, and I took the liberty to conclude that if I did live till that time, he would make his appearance. But I do not say whether he will make his appearance or I shall go where he is.[115]

---

[112]Letter to Presendia Huntington Buell, 15 March 1839; *PWJS,* 387.

[113]Discourse of 2 April 1843, recorded by William Clayton; *WJS,* 168–69; D&C 130:14–17.

[114]Discourse of 2 April 1843, recorded by Willard Richards; *WJS,* 172; see D&C 130:14–15.

[115]Discourse of 6 April 1843, recorded by Willard Richards; *WJS,* 179; see D&C 130:14–16.

Christ says, "No man knoweth the day or the hour when the Son of Man cometh." . . . Did Christ speak this as a general principle throughout all generations? Oh no; he spoke in the present tense. No man that was then living upon the footstool of God knew the day or the hour. But he did not say that there was no man throughout all generations that should know the day or the hour. No, for this would be in flat contradiction with other scripture, for the prophet says that God will do nothing but what he will reveal unto his servants the prophets [Amos 3:7]. Consequently, if it is not made known to the prophets it will not come to pass.[116]

The rainbow is not to be seen. It is a sign of the commencement of famine, pestilence, and so forth, and that the coming of the Messiah is not far distant.[117]

So long as you see the rainbow stretching across the heavens, there will be seed time and harvest, and the Son of Man will not come that year.[118]

While inquiring of the Lord concerning the end of time, it was made known to me by the Holy Spirit that there should be prosperity, seed time, and harvest every year in which the rainbow was seen. For to that was Noah referred as a surety on this subject. But in the year when the bow was not to be seen would commence desolation, calamity, and distress among the nations, without seed time or harvest.[119]

So long as we see the bow in the cloud, seed time and harvest shall continue that year. When the bow shall cease, then shall come famine, wars, and so forth, after which the sign of the Son of Man shall be seen in heaven.[120]

---

[116]Discourse of 6 April 1843, recorded by James Burgess; *WJS,* 180–81.

[117]Discourse of 10 March 1844, recorded by Thomas Bullock; *WJS,* 336.

[118]Discourse of 10 March 1844, recorded by James Burgess; *WJS,* 334.

[119]Discourse of 10 March 1844, recorded by John Solomon Fullmer; *WJS,* 336.

[120]Discourse of 10 March 1844, recorded by Franklin D. Richards; *WJS,* 335.

The Savior will not come this year, nor forty years to come. The bow has been seen in the cloud, and in that year that the bow is seen, seed time and harvest will be. But when the bow ceases to be seen, look out for a famine.[121]

I have asked of the Lord concerning his coming, and while asking, the Lord gave me a sign and said: "In the days of Noah I set a bow in the heavens as a sign and token that in any year that the bow should be seen, the Lord would not come; but there should be seed time [and] harvest during that year. But whenever you see the bow withdraw, it shall be a token that there shall be famine, pestilence, and great distress among the nations." . . .

Jesus Christ never did reveal to any man the precise time that he would come. Go and read the scriptures, and you cannot find anything that specified the exact [time] he would come. All that say so are false teachers.[122]

Matthew 25:14–30

The reflection that everyone is to receive according to his own diligence and perseverance while in the vineyard ought to inspire everyone who is called to be a minister of these glad tidings to so improve his talent that he may gain other talents, that when the Master sits down to take an account of the conduct of his servants, that it may be said, "Well done, good and faithful servant; thou hast been faithful over a few things, I will now make thee ruler over many things: enter thou into the joy of thy lord."[123]

Without a strict observance of all [God's] divine requirements, you may at last be found wanting. And if so, you will

---

[121]Discourse of 10 March 1844, recorded by Willard Richards; *WJS*, 335.

[122]Discourse of 10 March 1844, recorded by Wilford Woodruff; *WJS*, 332.

[123]*Evening and Morning Star*, February 1834, 135.

admit that your lot will be cast among the unprofitable servants. We beseech you therefore, brethren, to improve upon all things committed to your charge, that you lose not your reward.[124]

The great plan of salvation is a theme which ought to occupy our strictest attention and be regarded as one of heaven's best gifts to mankind. No consideration whatever ought to deter us from approving ourselves in the sight of God, according to his divine requirement. Men not infrequently forget that they are dependent upon heaven for every blessing which they are permitted to enjoy and that for every opportunity granted them they are to give an account. You know, brethren, that when the Master called his servants he gave them their several benefits to improve on while he should tarry for a little season, and then he will call each to render his account. And where five talents were bestowed, ten will be required, and he that has made no improvement will be cast out as an unprofitable servant, and the faithful are to enjoy everlasting honors. Therefore, we earnestly implore the grace of our Father to rest upon you, through Jesus Christ his Son, that you may not faint in the hour of temptation, nor be overcome in the time of persecution.[125]

Blessings offered but rejected are no longer blessings but become like the talent hid in the earth by the wicked and slothful servant. The proffered good returns to the giver; the blessing is bestowed on those who will receive and occupy. For unto him that hath shall be given, and he shall have abundantly; but from him that hath not, or will not receive, shall be taken away that which he hath, or might have had.[126]

---

[124]*Evening and Morning Star,* March 1834, 142.

[125]*Evening and Morning Star,* April 1834, 152.

[126]Letter to Nancy Rigdon, *Sangamo Journal,* 19 August 1842; *PWJS,* 509.

Matthew 27:1

Darkness prevails at this time as it was at the time Jesus Christ was about to be crucified. The powers of darkness strove to obscure the glorious sun of righteousness that began to dawn upon the world and was soon to burst in great blessings upon the heads of the faithful.[127]

Matthew 27:52–53

We read that many bodies of the Saints arose at Christ's resurrection, probably all the Saints.[128]

Matthew 28:18

Did ever language of such magnitude fall from the lips of any man? Hearken [to] him![129]

---

[127]Journal, 12 November 1835; *PJS*, 2:75; cf. *PJS*, 1:133.

[128]Discourse of 16 May 1841, reported in *Times and Seasons*, 1 June 1841, 429.

[129]Discourse of 27 August 1843, recorded by James Burgess; *WJS*, 246.

Mark

Mark 1:2–5

See under Matthew 3:1–6.

Mark 1:4

It was the baptism of repentance unto the remission of sins for the receiving of the Holy Ghost, and it was the gospel baptism.[1]

John preached the gospel and must have preached the first principles. If so he must have preached the doctrine of baptism for the remission of sins, for that is the first principle of the gospel and was ordained before the foundation of the world.[2]

John came preaching the gospel for the remission of sins. He had his authority from God, and the oracles of God were with him. The kingdom of [God] for a season seemed to be with John alone. . . . He preached the same gospel and baptism that Jesus and the apostles preached after him.[3]

Mark 1:7–8

See under Luke 3:16.

Mark 1:10

See under Matthew 3:16.

Mark 1:19

See under Matthew 4:21.

---

[1]Discourse of 17 January 1843, recorded by Wilford Woodruff; *WJS*, 155.

[2]Discourse of 22 January 1843, recorded by William Clayton; *WJS*, 159.

[3]Discourse of 22 January 1843, recorded by Wilford Woodruff; *WJS*, 156–58.

Mark 2:15–17

Christ said he came to call sinners to repentance and save them. Christ was condemned by the righteous Jews because he took sinners into his society. He took them upon the principle that they repented of their sins.[4]

Mark 3:28–29

See under Matthew 12:31–32; 2 Peter 1:10–11.

Mark 4:30–32

See under Matthew 13:31–32.

Mark 5:1–13

See under Matthew 8:28–34.

Mark 6:7

See under Matthew 10:1.

Mark 8:35–36

See under Matthew 10:39, JST; 16:25–26.

Mark 9:2–8

See under Matthew 17:1–8.

Mark 9:11–13

See under Matthew 11:13–15.

Mark 12:18–25

See under Luke 20:27–36.

---

[4]Discourse of 9 June 1842, recorded by Eliza R. Snow; *WJS,* 123.

Mark 13:7–8

See under Matthew 24:6–7, 12–13.

Mark 13:22

See under Matthew 24:24.

Mark 13:24–26

See under Matthew 24:27–30.

Mark 13:28–29

See under Matthew 24:32–33.

Mark 13:32

See under Matthew 24:36.

Mark 16:17–18

No matter who believeth, these signs, such as healing the sick, casting out devils, and so forth, should follow all that believe, whether male or female.[5]

They might attain unto these blessings by a virtuous life and conversation,[6] and diligence in keeping all the commandments.[7]

---

[5]Discourse of 28 April 1842, recorded by Eliza R. Snow; *WJS,* 115.

[6]The primary definition of *conversation* in Joseph Smith's day, as in the King James Translation of the Bible, was "general course of manners; behavior; deportment"; Noah Webster, *An American Dictionary of the English Language* (New York: S. Converse, 1828), s.v. "conversation."

[7]Discourse of 28 April 1842, recorded in the "Book of the Law of the Lord"; *WJS,* 119.

Luke

Luke 1:5–23

Zacharias pleaded with the Lord in the temple that he might have seed, so that the priesthood might be preserved.[1]

The priesthood was given to Aaron and his posterity throughout all generations. We can trace the lineage down to Zacharias, he being the only lawful administrator in his day. And the Jews knew it well, for they always acknowledged the priesthood. Zacharias, having no children, knew that the promise of God must fail. Consequently, he went into the temple to wrestle with God, according to the order of the priesthood, to obtain a promise of a son. And when the angel told him that his promise was granted, he, because of unbelief, was struck dumb.[2]

Luke 1:17

See under Matthew 3:1–6; 11:13–15.

Luke 3:3–4

See under Matthew 3:1–6; Mark 1:4.

Luke 3:8–9

See under Matthew 3:8–10.

Luke 3:16

John was a priest after the order of Aaron and had the keys of that priesthood. [He] came forth preaching repentance and baptism for the remission of sins but at the same time cried out, "There cometh one after me mightier than I, the latchet of whose shoes I am not worthy to unloose." Christ came according to the

---

[1]Discourse of 21 March 1841, recorded by William P. McIntire; *WJS*, 67.

[2]Discourse of 23 July 1843, recorded by James Burgess; *WJS*, 235.

word of John. He was greater than John, because he held the keys of the Melchizedek Priesthood and the kingdom of God and had before revealed the priesthood to Moses. Yet Christ was baptized by John to fulfill all righteousness.[3]

He told the people that his mission was to preach repentance and baptize with water, but it was he that should come after him that should baptize with fire and the Holy Ghost. If he had been an impostor, he might have gone to work beyond his bounds and undertaken to have performed ordinances that did not belong to that office and calling under the spirit of Elias. . . . John's mission was limited to preaching and baptizing, but what he did was legal. And when Jesus Christ came to any of John's disciples, he baptized them with fire and the Holy Ghost. We find the apostles endowed with greater power than John; their office was more under the spirit and power of Elijah than Elias. . . .

What I want to impress upon your minds is the difference of power in the different parts of the priesthood, so that when any man comes among you saying, "I have the spirit of Elias," you can know whether he be true or false. For any man that comes having the spirit and power of Elias will not transcend his bounds. John did not transcend his bound but faithfully performed that part belonging to his office. And every portion of the great building should be prepared rightly and assigned to its proper place. It is necessary to know who holds the keys of power and who does not, or we may be likely to be deceived. That person who holds the keys of Elias has a preparatory work.[4]

John says, "I baptize you with water, but when Jesus comes, who has the power, he shall administer the baptism of fire and the Holy Ghost." . . . John said his baptism was nothing without the baptism of Jesus Christ.[5]

---

[3]Discourse of 22 January 1843, recorded by Wilford Woodruff; *WJS*, 157–58.

[4]Discourse of 10 March 1844, recorded by Wilford Woodruff; *WJS*, 328.

[5]Discourse of 7 April 1844, recorded by Thomas Bullock; *KFD*, 79.

"I baptize you with water, but when Jesus comes, having the keys, he shall baptize you with the baptisms of fire and Holy Ghost."[6]

John says, "I baptize you with water, but when Jesus Christ comes he shall administer the baptism of fire and the Holy Ghost." John said his baptism was good for nothing without the baptism of Jesus Christ. Many talk of any baptism not being essential to salvation. But this would lay the foundation of their damnation.[7]

See also under Matthew 3:1–6; 11:13–15; John 3:3–5.

Luke 3:21–22
See under Matthew 3:16.

Luke 4:18
See under 1 Peter 3:18–19; 4:6.

Luke 5:29–32
See under Mark 2:15–17.

Luke 6:22
See under Matthew 5:10–12.

Luke 6:27–28
See under Matthew 5:43–45.

Luke 6:30
See under Matthew 5:42.

---

[6]Discourse of 7 April 1844, recorded by Willard Richards; *KFD,* 78.
[7]Discourse of 7 April 1844, recorded by Wilford Woodruff; *KFD,* 78.

Luke 6:43–45

Out of the abundance of the heart man speaks. The man that tells you words of life is the man that can save you.[8]

[The] best man brings forth [the] best works.[9]

Luke 7:28

See under Matthew 11:11.

Luke 8:26–39

See under Matthew 8:28–34.

Luke 9:1–2

See under Matthew 10:1.

Luke 9:24–25

See under Matthew 10:39, JST; 16:25–26.

Luke 9:28–36

See under Matthew 17:1–8.

Luke 11:28

As a church and a people it behooves us to be wise, and to seek to know the will of God and then be willing to do it. For "blessed is he that heareth the word of the Lord and keepeth it," says the scripture.[10]

Luke 12:10

See under Matthew 12:31–32.

---

[8]Discourse of 7 April 1844, recorded by Thomas Bullock; *KFD,* 69.

[9]Discourse of 7 April 1844, recorded by Willard Richards; *KFD,* 68.

[10]*Times and Seasons,* 15 July 1842, 857.

Luke 13:1–5

See under Job 4–37.

Luke 13:34

See under Matthew 23:37–38.

Luke 15:1–2

What is the rule of interpretation? Just no interpretation at all, understood precisely as it reads. I have a key by which I understand the scripture: I inquire what was the question which drew out the answer. . . . First dig up the root. What drew the saying out of Jesus? Pharisees and scribes murmured: "This man receiveth sinners, and eateth with them." This is the key word— to answer the murmuring and questioning of Sadducees and Pharisees: "Is this man as great as he pretends to be and eats with publicans and sinners?"[11]

Luke 15:2–10

"This man receiveth sinners." He spoke this parable: "What man of you, having a hundred sheep and a hundred Sadducees and Pharisees . . . ?" "If you Pharisees and Sadducees are in the sheepfold, I have no mission for you. [I am] sent to look up sheep that are lost. [I] will back them up and make joy in heaven, hunting after a few individuals, laying [them] on [my] shoulder, one publican you despise, one piece of silver, the piece which was lost. Joy is found [in the presence] of the angels over one sinner that repenteth."

[The Pharisees and Sadducees are] so righteous they will be damned. Anyhow, you cannot save them; [it is like] rain off from a goose's back. "Great I, little you!"[12]

---

[11]Discourse of 29 January 1843, recorded by Willard Richards; *WJS,* 161.

[12]Discourse of 29 January 1843, recorded by Willard Richards; *WJS,* 161.

Luke 15:11–32

"A certain man had two sons," and so forth. "[I] am a poor publican, a sinner." [He] humbled [himself], spending [his] bread and living. "I'll return to my father's house, to Jesus." "You Pharisees [are] so righteous you cannot be touched." "I will arise and claim not [to] be a Pharisee or Sadducee. I claim not to be a son. Do not let me starve." . . . All that is meant is brought to bear upon the Pharisee, Sadducee, the publican, and sinners. [The] eldest son: Pharisees and Sadducees murmuring and complaining because Jesus sat with publicans and sinners. . . .

[The] dealing of God with individual men [is] always righteous. [They] always have access to [the] throne of God. . . . Servants of God of the last days, myself and those I have ordained, have the priesthood and a mission—to the publicans and sinners.[13]

Luke 16:16

He, having received the holy anointing, was the only lawful administrator, and the Jews all knew it. For "the law and the prophets were until John; since then the kingdom of heaven is preached, and all men press into it." Why? Because John was the only lawful administrator, and they, the Jews, well knew it. Consequently, the only alternative was for them to yield obedience to [the] mandates of this wild man of the woods, namely John, or be damned.[14]

Luke 16:31

The victims of priestcraft and superstition would not believe though one should rise from the dead.[15]

---

[13]Discourse of 29 January 1843, recorded by Willard Richards; *WJS,* 161–62.

[14]Discourse of 23 July 1843, recorded by James Burgess; *WJS,* 235.

[15]Journal, 12 December 1835; *PJS,* 2:102.

Priestcraft has its victims also in this age, like those in ages past, that would not believe though one should rise from the dead.[16]

Luke 18:1–8

[When] all things else fail you but God alone, and you continue to weary him with your importunings, as the poor woman the unjust judge, he will not fail to execute judgement upon your enemies and to avenge his own elect that cry unto him day and night. Behold, he will not fail you.[17]

Luke 18:10–14

The better a man is the more his prayer will prevail, like the publican and Pharisee. One was justified rather than the other, showing that both were justified in a degree.[18]

Luke 20:27–36

A man must enter into an everlasting covenant with his wife in this world, or he will have no claim on her in the next.[19]

No man can obtain an eternal blessing unless the contract or covenant be made in view of eternity. All contracts in view of this life only terminate with this life. [Such is the] case of the woman and seven husbands. Those who keep no eternal law in this life or make no eternal contract are single and alone in the eternal world and are only made angels to minister to those who shall be heirs of salvation, never becoming sons of God, having never kept the law of God, that is, eternal law.[20]

---

[16]1834–36 History, 12 December 1835; *PJS,* 1:158.

[17]Letter to Edward Partridge, W. W. Phelps, John Whitmer, Algernon Sidney Gilbert, John Corrill, Isaac Morley and all the Saints whom it may concern, from Kirtland Mills, Ohio, 10 December 1833; *PWJS,* 310.

[18]Statement of 24 December 1842, recorded by Willard Richards; *PJS,* 3.

[19]Discourse of 16 July 1843, recorded by William Clayton; *WJS,* 233.

[20]Discourse of 16 July 1843, recorded by Franklin D. Richards; *WJS,* 232.

Luke 21:9–11

See under Matthew 24:6–7, 12–13.

Luke 21:25–27

See under Matthew 24:27–30.

Luke 21:29–31

See under Matthew 24:32–33.

Luke 21:36

"Watch and pray always," says our Savior, "that ye may be accounted worthy to escape the things that are coming on the earth, and to stand before the Son of Man." If Enoch, Abraham, Moses, the children of Israel, and all God's people were saved by keeping the commandments of God, we, if saved at all, shall be saved upon the same principle. As God governed Abraham, Isaac, and Jacob as families, and the children of Israel as a nation, so we as a Church must be under his guidance if we are prospered, preserved, and sustained. Our only confidence can be in God, our only wisdom obtained from him, and he alone must be our protector and safeguard, spiritually and temporally, or we fall.[21]

Luke 22:3–4

From apostates the faithful have received the severest persecutions. Judas was rebuked and immediately betrayed his Lord into the hands of his enemies, because Satan entered into him. There is a supreme intelligence bestowed upon such as obey the gospel with full purpose of heart, which, if sinned against, the apostates are left naked and destitute of the Spirit of God, and they are, in truth, nigh unto cursing, and their end is to be burned. When once that light which was in them is taken from them, they become as much darkened as they were previously enlightened.

---

[21]*Times and Seasons,* 15 July 1842, 857.

And then, no marvel if all their power should be enlisted against the truth, and they, Judas-like, seek the destruction of those who were their greatest benefactors. What nearer friend on earth or in heaven had Judas than the Savior? And his first object was to destroy him! Who among all the Saints in these last days can consider himself as good as our Lord? Who is as perfect, who is as pure, and who as holy as he was? Are they to be found? He never transgressed or broke a commandment or law of heaven. No deceit was in his mouth, neither was guile found in his heart. And yet one that ate with him, who had often supped of the same cup, was the first to lift up his heel against him. Where is there one like him? He cannot be found on earth. Then why should his followers complain if from those whom they once called brethren, and considered in the nearest relation in the everlasting covenant, they should receive persecution? From what source emanated the principle which has ever been manifested by apostates from the true Church to persecute with double diligence, and seek with double perseverance, to destroy those whom they once professed to love, with whom they once communed, and with whom they once covenanted to strive with every power in righteousness to obtain the rest of God? Perhaps, our brethren will say, the same that caused Satan to seek to overthrow the kingdom of God, because he himself was evil, and God's kingdom is holy.[22]

Luke 23:42–43

"Paradise" [is a] modern word [that] does not answer to the original word used by Jesus. . . . "This day you will be with me in the world of spirits, and then I will teach you all about it." . . . [It is] a world of departed spirits. Disembodied spirits all go— good, bad, and indifferent. Misery in [the] world of spirits is to know they come short of the glory others enjoy. They are their own accusers.[23]

---

[22]*Evening and Morning Star,* April 1834, 152.[22]*Evening and Morning Star,* April 1834, 152.

[23]Discourse of 11 June 1843, recorded by Willard Richards; *WJS,* 211.

I will say something about the spirits in prison. There has been much said about the saying of Jesus on the cross to the thief, saying, "This day thou shalt be with me in paradise." The commentators or translators make it out to say "paradise," but what is "paradise"? It is a modern word; it does not answer at all to the original that Jesus made use of. There is nothing in the original, in any language, that signifies "paradise." But it was "This day I will be with thee in the world of spirits and will teach thee, or answer thy inquiries." The thief on the cross was to be with Jesus Christ in the world of spirits. He did not say "paradise" or "heaven." . . .

There has been also much said about the word "hell," and the sectarian world have preached much about it. But what is hell? It is another modern term. It is taken from *hadēs,* the Greek, or *she'ôl,* the Hebrew. The true signification is a world of spirits. *Hadēs, she'ôl,* paradise, spirits in prison—[it] is all one. It is a world of spirits. The righteous and the wicked all go to the same world of spirits.[24]

Luke 24:36–40

Jesus showed himself to his disciples, and they thought it was his spirit. And they were afraid to approach his spirit.[25]

Luke 24:46–47

By this we learn that it behooved Christ to suffer and to be crucified and rise again on the third day, for the express purpose that repentance and remission of sins should be preached unto all nations.[26]

---

[24]Discourse of 11 June 1843, recorded by Wilford Woodruff; *WJS,* 213–14.

[25]Discourse of 9 October 1843, recorded by Willard Richards; *WJS,* 254.

[26]*Messenger and Advocate,* September 1835, 180–81.

John

John 1:6–8

See under John 1:19–20.

John 1:19–20

John was very particular to tell the people he was not that Light but was sent to bear witness of that Light.[1]

John 1:32–34

See under Matthew 3:16.

John 3:3–5

Baptism is a sign ordained of God for the believer in Christ to take upon himself in order to enter into the kingdom of God. For "except you are born of the water and the Spirit you cannot enter into the kingdom of God," saith the Savior, as it is a sign of command which God hath set for man to enter into this kingdom. Those who seek to enter in any other way will seek in vain, for God will not receive them, neither will the angels acknowledge their works as accepted. For they have not taken upon themselves those ordinances and signs which God ordained for man to receive in order to receive a celestial glory. And God has decreed that all who will not obey his voice shall not escape the damnation of hell. What is the damnation of hell? To go with that society who have not obeyed his commands.

Baptism is a sign to God, to angels, and to heaven, that we do the will of God, and there is no other way beneath the heavens whereby God hath ordained for man to come. Any other course is in vain. God hath decreed and ordained that man should repent of all his sins and be baptized for the remission of his sins.

---

[1]Discourse of 10 March 1844, recorded by Wilford Woodruff; *WJS*, 328.

Then he can come to God in the name of Jesus Christ, in faith. Then we have the promise of the Holy Ghost. . . . It mattereth not whether we live long or short after we come to a knowledge of these principles and obey them. I know that all men will be damned if they do not come in the way which God has appointed.[2]

This strong and positive answer of Jesus, as to water baptism, settles the question. If God is the same yesterday, today, and forever, it is no wonder he is so positive in the great declaration: "He that believes and is baptized shall be saved, and he that believes not shall be damned" [Mark 16:16]. There was no other name given under heaven, nor any other ordinance admitted, whereby men could be saved. No wonder the apostle said, being "buried with him in baptism," ye shall rise from the dead [Rom. 6:4].[3]

[One] might as well baptize a bag of sand as a man, if not done in view of the getting of the Holy Ghost. Baptism by water is but one-half a baptism and is good for nothing without the other, the Holy Ghost.[4]

[It is] one thing to see the kingdom and another to be in it. [One] must have a change of heart to see the kingdom of God and subscribe [to] the articles of adoption to enter therein.[5]

The baptism of water with the baptism of fire and the Holy Ghost attending it are necessary. [We] must be born of water and spirit in order to get into the kingdom of God.[6]

---

[2]Discourse of 20 March 1842, recorded by Wilford Woodruff; *WJS,* 107–9.

[3]*Times and Seasons,* 1 September 1842, 905.

[4]Discourse of 9 July 1843, recorded by Willard Richards; *WJS,* 230.

[5]Discourse of 15 October 1843, recorded by Willard Richards; *WJS,* 256.

[6]Discourse of 7 April 1844, recorded by Thomas Bullock; *KFD,* 79.

Baptism of water, fire, and Holy Ghost are inseparably connected.[7]

John 4:24

The Father has a body of flesh and bones as tangible as man's, the Son also, but the Holy Ghost is a personage of spirit. And a person cannot have the personage of the Holy Ghost in his heart. He may receive the gift of the Holy Ghost; it may descend upon him but not tarry with him.[8]

John 5:19

"I do the things I saw my Father do before worlds came rolling into existence. I saw my Father work out his kingdom with fear and trembling, and I must do the same. [Then] I shall give my kingdom to the Father so that he obtains kingdom rolling upon kingdom," so that Jesus treads in his tracks as he had gone before.[9]

What did Jesus do? "Why, I do the things that I saw the Father do when worlds came into existence. I saw the Father work out a kingdom with fear and trembling, and I can do the same. And when I get my kingdom worked [out], I will present [it] to the Father, and it will exalt his glory." And Jesus steps into his tracks to inherit what God did before.[10]

What did Jesus Christ do? "The same thing as I saw the Father do." Saw the Father do what? "Work out a kingdom. When I do so too, I will give [it] to the Father, which will add to

---

[7]Discourse of 7 April 1844, recorded by Willard Richards; *KFD,* 78.

[8]Discourse of 2 April 1843, recorded by Willard Richards; *WJS,* 173; see D&C 130:22–23.

[9]Discourse of 7 April 1844, recorded by Thomas Bullock; *KFD,* 33.

[10]Discourse of 7 April 1844, recorded by William Clayton; *KFD,* 32.

his glory. He will take a higher exaltation, and I will take his place and be also exalted."[11]

He laid down his life and took it up, same as his Father had done before. He did as he was sent, to lay down his life and take it up again.[12]

The Savior says, "The work that my Father did do I also." And these are the works: he took himself a body and then laid down his life that he might take it up again. . . . We then also took bodies to lay them down, to take them up again.[13]

See also under John 10:17–18.

John 5:26
See under John 10:17–18.

John 5:28–29
Some shall rise to the everlasting burning of God, and some shall rise to the damnation of their own filthiness—same as the lake of fire and brimstone.[14]

John 6:68
The Church of Jesus Christ of Latter-day Saints has the words of eternal life.[15]

John 8:56
See under Galatians 3:8.

---

[11]Discourse of 7 April 1844, recorded by Wilford Woodruff; *KFD*, 32.

[12]Discourse of 16 June 1844, recorded by Thomas Bullock; *WJS*, 380.

[13]Discourse of 16 June 1844, recorded by George Laub; *WJS*, 382.

[14]Discourse of 7 April 1844, recorded by Thomas Bullock; *KFD*, 81.

[15]*Times and Seasons,* 1 November 1843, 376.

John 10:17–18

As the Father hath power in himself, so the Son hath power in himself. Then the Father has some day laid down his body and taken it again, so he has a body of his own. So has his Son a body of his own. So each one will be in his own body.[16]

Jesus said: "As the Father hath power in himself, even so hath the Son power to do what the Father did." That answer is obvious: to lay down his body and take it up. Jesus did as [his] Father—laid down his body and took it up again.[17]

What did Jesus say? "As the Father hath power in himself, even so hath the Son power." To do what? Why, what the Father did, to lay down his body and take it up again. Jesus, what are you going to do? "To lay down my life as my Father did, that I might take it up again."[18]

Jesus said, "As the Father hath power in himself, even so hath the Son power to do what the Father did": lay down his body and take it up again.[19]

Jesus Christ said, "As the Father hath power in himself, so hath the Son power in himself." To do what? "[As] the Father did—even to lay down my body and take it up again."[20]

See also under John 5:19.

John 13:34–35

As the new commandment given anciently was to love one

---

[16]Discourse of 11 June 1843, recorded by Wilford Woodruff; *WJS*, 214.

[17]Discourse of 7 April 1844, recorded by Thomas Bullock; *KFD*, 31.

[18]Discourse of 7 April 1844, recorded by William Clayton; *KFD*, 30.

[19]Discourse of 7 April 1844, recorded by Willard Richards; *KFD*, 30.

[20]Discourse of 7 April 1844, recorded by Wilford Woodruff; *KFD*, 30.

another, even so the works of the Saints, at home and abroad, will bear their own testimony whether they love the brethren.[21]

John 14:2–3

From sundry revelations which had been received, it was apparent that many important points touching the salvation of man had been taken from the Bible, or lost before it was compiled. It appeared self evident from what truths were left that if God rewarded every one according to the deeds done in the body, the term "heaven," as intended for the Saints' eternal home, must include more kingdoms than one.[22]

"There are a great many mansions in my Father's house. I am going to prepare one for you, rather better than common." It is the privilege of the sons of God to inherit the same mansion. . . . If we should tell of different glories, as Paul did [1 Cor. 15:40–42], every man that receives the gospel receives that inheritance that the apostles did.[23]

The question is frequently asked, "Can we not be saved without going through with all these ordinances?" I would answer: No, not the fulness of salvation. Jesus said there were many mansions in his Father's house, and he would go and prepare a place for them. "House," here named, should have been translated "kingdom," and any person who is exalted to the highest mansion has to abide a celestial law—and the whole law too.[24]

We have reason to have the greatest hope and consolation for

---

[21]*Times and Seasons,* 1 November 1843, 376.

[22]1839 History; *PJS,* 1:372.

[23]Discourse of summer of 1839, recorded in Willard Richards's "Pocket Companion"; *WJS,* 13–14.

[24]Discourse of 21 January 1844, recorded by Wilford Woodruff; *WJS,* 319.

our dead. . . . For we have seen them walk in the midst and sink asleep in the arms of Jesus. Hence is the glory of the sun.[25]

What have we to console us in relation to our dead? We have the greatest hope in relation to our dead of any people on earth. We have seen them walk worthy on earth, and those who have died in the faith are now in the Celestial kingdom of God.[26]

It should be, "In my Father's kingdom are many kingdoms, in order that ye may be heirs of God and joint heirs with me." I do not believe the Methodist doctrine of sending honest men and noble-minded men to hell, along with the murderer and adulterer. . . . There are many mansions for those who obey a celestial law, and there are other mansions for those who come short of that law—every man in his own order.[27]

"In my Father's house, or kingdom, are many kingdoms or worlds. I will go to prepare a place for you. And according to your works you shall be rewarded."[28]

"In my Father's kingdom are many kingdoms. I go to prepare a kingdom for you, that the exaltation that I receive, you may receive also."[29]

John 14:12–14

"He that believeth—any person that believes—the works I do shall he do also, and greater works." The Father could not be glorified in the Son on any other principle than [our] coming to

---

[25]Discourse of 7 April 1844, recorded by Thomas Bullock; *KFD,* 71.

[26]Discourse of 7 April 1844, recorded by Wilford Woodruff; *KFD,* 70.

[27]Discourse of 12 May 1844, recorded by Thomas Bullock; *WJS,* 367–68.

[28]Discourse of 12 May 1844, recorded by George Laub; *WJS,* 370.

[29]Discourse of 12 May 1844, recorded by Samuel W. Richards; *WJS,* 371.

God, asking, receiving, [having the] heavens open, [seeing] visions, and so forth. They are done away because of unbelief.[30]

John 14:16–26

There are two Comforters spoken of. [The first] is the Holy Ghost, the same as given on the day of Pentecost and that all Saints receive after faith, repentance, and baptism. This first Comforter, or Holy Ghost, has no other effect than pure intelligence. . . .

The other Comforter spoken of is a subject of great interest and perhaps understood by few of this generation. After a person hath faith in Christ, repents of his sins, is baptized for the remission of his sins, and received the Holy Ghost (by the laying on of hands), which is the first Comforter, then let him continue to humble himself before God, hungering and thirsting after righteousness and living by every word of God. The Lord will soon say unto him, "Son, thou shalt be exalted." When the Lord has thoroughly proved him and finds that the man is determined to serve him at all hazards, then the man will find his calling and election made sure. Then it will be his privilege to receive the other Comforter, which the Lord hath promised the Saints.

Now what is this other Comforter? It is no more or less than the Lord Jesus Christ himself. And this is the sum and substance of the whole matter, that when any man obtains this last Comforter he will have the personage of Jesus Christ to attend him or appear unto him from time to time. Even he will manifest the Father unto him, and they will take up their abode with him. The visions of the heavens will be opened unto him, the Lord will teach him face to face, and he may have a perfect knowledge of the mysteries of the kingdom of God. This is the state and place the ancient Saints arrived at when they had such glorious visions: Isaiah, Ezekiel, John upon the Isle of Patmos, St. Paul in

---

[30]Discourse of summer of 1839, recorded in Willard Richards's "Pocket Companion"; *WJS,* 14.

the third heavens, and all the Saints who held communion with the General Assembly and Church of the Firstborn.[31]

There is one Comforter, and another Comforter to abide with you forever. Reach to things within the veil. Know that you are sealed. If you get it, it will stand by you forever. How is it obtained? "Keep my commandments. . . ." It is a privilege to view the Son of Man himself. "He dwelleth with you, and shall be in you." His Spirit shall be in you. "I will not have you comfortless. I will come to you, abide with you forever, and seal you up to eternal life."[32]

The other Comforter spoken of [in] John is Jesus himself, [who] is to come and take up his abode with them.[33]

See also under Jeremiah 31:34.

John 14:21

"I will manifest myself to him." If he does not, he has not told the truth.[34]

John 14:23

There are certain characters that walked with God, saw him, conversed about heaven, and so forth.[35]

The appearing of the Father and the Son in John 14:23 is a

---

[31]Discourse of 27 June 1839, recorded in Willard Richards's "Pocket Companion"; *WJS*, 4–5.

[32]Discourse of summer of 1839, recorded in Willard Richards's "Pocket Companion"; *WJS*, 14.

[33]Discourse of 30 March 1841, recorded by William P. McIntire; *WJS*, 68.

[34]Discourse of summer of 1839, recorded in Willard Richards's "Pocket Companion"; *WJS*, 14.

[35]Discourse of summer of 1839, recorded in Willard Richards's "Pocket Companion"; *WJS*, 14.

personal appearing, and the idea that they will dwell in a man's heart is a sectarian doctrine and is false.[36]

The appearing of the Father and of the Son in that verse is a personal appearance. To say that the Father and the Son dwell in a man's heart is an old sectarian notion and is not correct.[37]

John 14:26

"But the Comforter that I will send"—not the other Comforter—"shall teach you all things." Who? "He that loveth me." "This [Comforter] shall bring all things to remembrance, whatsoever things I have said unto you. He shall teach you until ye come to me and my Father." God is not a respecter of persons; we all have the same privilege. Come to God! Weary him until he blesses you. We are entitled to the same blessings: Jesus, revelations, just men, and angels. Not laying again the doctrine of Christ, go on unto perfection. Obtain that Holy Spirit of Promise, then you can be sealed to eternal life.[38]

No man can receive the Holy Ghost without receiving revelations. The Holy Ghost is a revelator.[39]

John 15:1–8

If we kept the commandments of God, we should bring forth fruit, be the friends of God, and know what our Lord did.[40]

---

[36]Discourse of 2 April 1843, recorded by William Clayton; *WJS*, 169; see D&C 130:3.

[37]Discourse of 2 April 1843, recorded by Willard Richards; *WJS*, 171; see D&C 130:3.

[38]Discourse of summer of 1839, recorded in Willard Richards's "Pocket Companion"; *WJS*, 14–15.

[39]Discourse of 15 October 1843, recorded by Willard Richards; *WJS*, 256.

[40]Discourse of 19 December 1841, recorded by Wilford Woodruff; *WJS*, 80–81.

John 15:12–13

"Why is it this babbler [Joseph Smith] gains so many followers and retains them?" Because I possess the principle of love. All I can offer the world [is] a good heart and a good hand. Mormons can testify whether I am willing to lay down my life for a Mormon. If it has been demonstrated that I have been willing to die for a Mormon, I am bold to declare before heaven that I am just as ready to die for a Presbyterian, a Baptist, or any other denomination.[41]

John 15:20

The trials [the Saints] have had to pass through shall work together for their good and prepare them for the society of those who have come up out of great tribulation, washed their robes, and made them white in the blood of the Lamb. Marvel not then if you are persecuted, but remember the words of the Savior, "The servant is not above his Lord; if they have persecuted me, they will persecute you also," and that all the afflictions through which the Saints have to pass are in fulfillment of the words of the prophets which have spoken since the world began. . . . Afflictions, persecutions, imprisonments, and deaths we must expect according to the scriptures.[42]

John 16:7–8

It ought to read thus: "And he shall remind the world of sin, and of righteousness, and of judgment." This Comforter reminds of these things through the servants of the Lord.[43]

This is [a] wrong translation, for to "remind" is correct.[44]

---

[41]Discourse of 9 July 1843, recorded by Willard Richards; *WJS*, 229.

[42]*Times and Seasons*, November 1839, 8–9.

[43]Discourse of 30 March 1841, recorded by William P. McIntire; *WJS*, 68.

[44]Discourse of 12 May 1844, recorded by George Laub; *WJS*, 371.

John 17:3

Eternal life is to know the only true God and his son Jesus, without which there is no salvation.[45]

Make your calling and election sure. Go on from grace to grace until you obtain a promise from God for yourselves that you shall have eternal life. This is eternal life, to know God and his son Jesus Christ. It is to be sealed up unto eternal life and obtain a promise for our posterity.[46]

There are very few who understand rightly the character of God. . . . What kind of a being is God? I again repeat the question. What kind of a being is God? Does any man or woman know? Have any of you seen him, heard him, communed with him? Here is the question that will peradventure from this time henceforth occupy your attention. The apostle says this is eternal life, to know God and Jesus Christ whom he has sent. That is eternal life. If any man inquire what kind of a being God is, if he will search diligently his own heart, [he will know] that unless he knows God he has no eternal life.[47]

[There are] few beings in the world who understand the character of God. [They] do not comprehend their own character. . . . What kind of a being is God? Ask yourselves. I repeat the question. What kind of a being is God? [Is there] any man or woman that knows? [Have] any of you seen him, heard him, communed with him? Here [is] a subject that will peradventure occupy your attention while you live. The apostle says this is eternal life, to "know thee the only true God, and Jesus Christ, whom thou hast sent." That is eternal life. If any man inquires what kind of being God is [and] casts his mind to know if the declaration of the

---

[45]Discourse of 13 August 1843, recorded by Martha Jane Coray; *WJS,* 241.

[46]Discourse of 10 March 1844, recorded by James Burgess; *WJS,* 334.

[47]Discourse of 7 April 1844, recorded by Thomas Bullock; *KFD,* 19, 21, 31.

apostle be true, he will realize that he has not eternal life. There can be eternal life on no other principle.[48]

To know God, learn to become Gods.[49]

If men do not comprehend the character of God, they do not comprehend themselves. What kind of a being is God? Eternal life [is] to know God. If man does not know God, [he] has not eternal life.[50]

But few understand the character of God. They do not know, they do not understand their relationship to God. . . . What kind of a being is God? Turn your thoughts in your hearts and say, have any of you seen or heard him or communed with him? This is a question that may occupy your attention. The scriptures inform us that this is eternal life, to know the only wise God and Jesus Christ whom he has sent. If any inquire what kind of a being God is, I would say if you don't know God, you have not eternal life. Go back and find out what kind of being God is.[51]

John 17:9–11

Men say there is one God: the Father, Son, and the Holy Ghost are only one God. It is a strange God anyhow, three in one and one in three. It is a curious thing anyhow. . . . I want to read the text to you myself: "I am agreed with the Father, and the Father is agreed with me, and we are agreed as one." The Greek shows that it should be "agreed." "Father, I pray for them that thou hast given me out of the world, . . . that they may be agreed and all come to dwell in unity and in all the glory and everlasting

---

[48]Discourse of 7 April 1844, recorded by William Clayton; *KFD,* 18, 20.

[49]Discourse of 7 April 1844, recorded by Samuel W. Richards; *WJS,* 361.

[50]Discourse of 7 April 1844, recorded by Willard Richards; *KFD,* 18, 20.

[51]Discourse of 7 April 1844, recorded by Wilford Woodruff; *KFD,* 18, 20.

burnings of God." And then we shall see as we are seen and be as God.[52]

"That we might be one," or to say, "be of one mind in the unity of the faith." But everyone [is] a different or separate person, and so [are] God, and Jesus Christ, and the Holy Ghost separate persons. But they all agree in one or the selfsame thing. But the Holy Ghost is yet a spiritual body and [is] waiting to take to himself a body, as the Savior did or as God did or the Gods before them took bodies.[53]

John 17:17

As [Jesus] says, "thy word is truth," so if we keep his word [we] shall all be actuated by the same principles [and] be as one man. And as angels are obedient to the same word, we shall have concourse to them and also to all the heavenly throng.[54]

John 17:21–22

See under John 17:9–11.

John 21:20–23

John the Revelator [is] among the ten tribes of Israel who had been led away by Shalmaneser, king of Assyria, to prepare them for their return from their long dispersion, to again possess the land of their fathers.[55]

------

[52]Discourse of 16 June 1844, recorded by Thomas Bullock; *WJS*, 380.

[53]Discourse of 16 June 1844, recorded by George Laub; *WJS*, 382.

[54]Discourse of 5 January 1841, recorded by William P. McIntire; *WJS*, 61.

[55]Discourse of 3 June 1831; John Whitmer, "The Book of John Whitmer, Kept by Commandment"; *An Early Latter Day Saint History*, ed. F. Mark McKiernan and Roger D. Launius (Independence, Mo.: Herald House, 1980), 66. The original manuscript incorrectly reads "Israel" instead of "Assyria." See also D&C 7.

Acts

Acts 1:4–5

When the apostles were raised up, they worked in Jerusalem, and Jesus commanded them to tarry there until they were endowed with power from on high. Had they not work to do in Jerusalem? They did work and prepared a people for the Pentecost. The kingdom of God was with them before the day of Pentecost, as well as afterwards. . . . The endowment was to prepare the disciples for their mission into the world.[1]

Acts 2:1–3

At one time God obtained a house, where Peter washed and anointed, and so forth, on the day of Pentecost.[2]

Acts 2:4–12

See under 1 Corinthians 14:2–33.

Acts 2:13

If we had the testimony of the Scribes and Pharisees concerning the outpouring of the Spirit on the day of Pentecost, they would have told us that it was no gift, but that the people were "drunken with new wine."[3]

Acts 2:25–30

David could not obtain celestial glory, and the reason why he had any hope, or obtained a promise that of his seed one should

---

[1]Discourse of 22 January 1843, recorded by Wilford Woodruff; *WJS*, 158.
[2]Discourse of 11 June 1843, recorded by Willard Richards; *WJS*, 211.
[3]*Times and Seasons*, 15 June 1842, 825.

be raised up to reign over Israel forever, was because he had not spoken against the Spirit. And because he had not done this, he obtained promise that God would not leave his soul in Hell.[4]

Acts 2:29, 34

Peter had the keys of eternal judgment. And he saw David in Hell and knew for what reason, and that David would have to remain there until the resurrection at the coming of Christ.[5]

Even David must wait for those times of refreshing [Acts 3:19–20] before he can come forth and his sins be blotted out. For Peter speaking of him says, "David hath not yet ascended into heaven, for his sepulchre is with us to this day." His remains were then in the tomb. Now we read that many bodies of the Saints arose at Christ's resurrection, probably all the Saints. But it seems that David did not. Why? Because he had been a murderer.[6]

See also under 2 Samuel 12:7–13; Acts 3:19–20.

Acts 2:38–39

By this we learn that the promise of the Holy Ghost is unto as many as the doctrine of repentance was to be preached, which was unto all nations. And we discover also that the promise was to extend by lineage, for Peter says, "not only unto you, but unto your children and unto all that are afar off." From this we infer that it was to continue unto their children's children, and even unto as many generations as should come after, even as many as the Lord their God should call. . . .

We learn from Peter that remission of sins is obtained by

---

[4]Discourse of 10 March 1844, recorded by Franklin D. Richards; *WJS,* 335.

[5]Discourse of 16 May 1841, recorded by William Clayton; *WJS,* 74.

[6]Discourse of 16 May 1841, reported in *Times and Seasons,* 1 June 1841, 429–30.

baptism in the name of the Lord Jesus Christ, and the gift of the Holy Ghost follows inevitably. For, says Peter, "you shall receive the gift of the Holy Ghost." Therefore, we believe in preaching the doctrine of repentance in all the world, both to old and young, rich and poor, bond and free. . . . In order to be benefitted by the doctrine of repentance, we must believe in obtaining the remission of sins. And in order to obtain the remission of sins, we must believe in the doctrine of baptism in the name of the Lord Jesus Christ. And if we believe in baptism for the remission of sins, we may expect a fulfillment of the promise of the Holy Ghost, for the promise extends to all whom the Lord our God shall call.[7]

Here you see the doctrine of repentance, baptism for the remission of sins, and the gift of the Holy Ghost, connected by the promise inseparably. Now I want you to consider the high standing of Peter. He was now being endowed with power from on high and held the keys of the kingdom of heaven. . . . This was the character that made the glorious promise of the gift of the Holy Ghost, predicated upon the baptism for the remission of sins. And he did not say that it was confined to that generation, but see further: "For the promise is unto you, and your children, and to all who are afar off, even as many as the Lord our God shall call." Then, if the callings of God extend unto us, we come within the purview of Peter's promise.[8]

What if we should attempt to get the Holy Ghost through any other means except the sign or way which God hath appointed? Should we obtain it? Certainly not; all other means would fail. The Lord says, "Do so and so, and I will bless so and so." There are certain key words and signs belonging to the priesthood which must be observed in order to obtain the blessings. The sign

---

[7]*Messenger and Advocate,* September 1835, 181.

[8]Letter to Isaac Galland, from Liberty Jail, Missouri, 22 March 1839; *Times and Seasons,* February 1840, 55.

of Peter was to repent and be baptized for the remission of sins, with the promise of the gift of the Holy Ghost. And in no other way is the gift of the Holy Ghost obtained.[9]

Here one of the witnesses says in so many words, "Repent, and be baptized." And we are of the opinion that Peter, having been taught by the Lord and commissioned by the Lord and endowed by the Lord, would be about as correct a counselor or ambassador as we or they could inquire of to know the right way to enter into the kingdom.[10]

See also under John 3:3–5.

Acts 3:17

Peter preached repentance and baptism for the remission of sins to the Jews, who had been led to acts of violence and blood by their leaders. But to the rulers he said, "I would that through ignorance ye did it, as did also those ye ruled."[11]

[Concerning the rulers of the Jews and Peter's preaching:] "I wot (wish) that through ignorance ye did it, as did those over whom ye ruled."[12]

Acts 3:19–20

Peter shows . . . that a murderer could not be redeemed until [God] would send Jesus Christ. . . . That is, that faith, repentance, and baptism would not save them until the[y were] scourged in Hell or paid the last farthing.[13]

---

[9]Discourse of 20 March 1842, recorded by Wilford Woodruff; *WJS,* 108.

[10]*Times and Seasons,* 1 September 1842, 904.

[11]Discourse of 16 May 1841, reported in *Times and Seasons,* 1 June 1841, 429.

[12]Discourse of 10 March 1844, recorded by Franklin D. Richards; *WJS,* 335.

[13]Discourse of 12 January 1841, recorded by William P. McIntire; *WJS,* 62.

Remission of sins by baptism was not to be preached to murderers. All the priests in Christendom might pray for a murderer on the scaffold forever but could not avail so much as a gnat towards his forgiveness. There is no forgiveness for murderers. They will have to wait until the time of redemption shall come, and that in Hell.[14]

The time of redemption here has reference to the time when Christ should come. Then and not till then would their sins be blotted out. Why? Because they were murderers, and no murderer hath eternal life. . . . If the ministers of religion had a proper understanding of the doctrine of eternal judgment, they would not be found attending the man who had forfeited his life to the injured laws of his country by shedding innocent blood. For such characters cannot be forgiven until they have paid the last farthing. The prayers of all the ministers in the world could never close the gates of Hell against a murderer.[15]

He did not say to them, "Repent and be baptized for the remission of your sins." But he said, "Repent therefore and be converted. . . ." This is the case with murderers. They could not be baptized for the remission of sins, for they had shed innocent blood.[16]

Acts 4:12

In the former ages of the world, before the Savior came in the flesh, the Saints were baptized in the name of Jesus Christ to come, because there never was any other name whereby men could be saved. And after he came in the flesh and was crucified, then the Saints were baptized in the name of Jesus Christ—

---

[14]Discourse of 16 May 1841, recorded by William Clayton; *WJS*, 74.

[15]Discourse of 16 May 1841, reported in *Times and Seasons*, 1 June 1841, 429–30.

[16]Discourse of 10 March 1844, recorded by Wilford Woodruff; *WJS*, 331.

crucified, risen from the dead, and ascended into heaven—that they might be buried in baptism like him, and be raised in glory like him.[17]

Acts 5:30–32

We are reminded of the words of Peter to the Jewish Sanhedrin, when speaking of Christ. He says that God raised him from the dead, "and we [the apostles] are his witnesses of these things, and so is also the Holy Ghost, whom God had given to them that obey him." So that after the testimony of the scriptures on this point, the assurance is given by the Holy Ghost, bearing witness to those who obey him, that Christ himself has assuredly risen from the dead.[18]

Acts 7:55–56

Stephen saw the Son of Man. [He] saw the Son of Man standing on the right hand of God. [There are] three personages in heaven who hold the keys—one to preside over all.[19]

Stephen says that Jesus Christ sat on the right hand of God. Any person that has seen the heavens opened knows that there are three personages in the heavens holding the keys of power.[20]

Acts 8:5–17

Philip was clothed with the power of Elias. When he went to Samaria, he could baptize for remission of sins but could not lay

---

[17]*Times and Seasons,* 1 September 1842, 905.

[18]*Evening and Morning Star,* March 1834, 144.

[19]Discourse of 11 June 1843, recorded by Willard Richards; *WJS,* 212.

[20]Discourse of 11 June 1843, recorded by Wilford Woodruff; *WJS,* 214. The manuscript reads "Peter" instead of "Stephen." But the combined evidence of the accounts of Elders Richards and Woodruff shows that "Stephen" was intended.

on hands for the gift of the Holy Ghost. But [he] sent for Peter and John, who had the power of Elijah.[21]

In the case of Philip, when he went down to Samaria [he] was under the spirit of Elias. He baptized both men and women. When Peter and John heard of it, they went down and laid hands on them, and they received the Holy Ghost. This shows the distinction between the two powers.[22]

Acts 9:1–2

Paul is about five feet high, [with] very dark hair, dark complexion, dark skin, large Roman nose, sharp face, small black eyes—penetrating as eternity, round shoulders, and a whining voice, except when elevated, and then it almost resembles the roaring of a lion. He was a good orator.[23]

Acts 9:3–6

Jesus himself, when he appeared to Paul on his way to Damascus, did not inform him how he could be saved. . . . Paul could not learn so much from the Lord relative to his duty in the common salvation of man as he could from one of Christ's ambassadors, called with the same heavenly calling of the Lord and endowed with the same power from on high so that what they loosed on earth should be loosed in heaven and what they bound on earth should be bound in heaven—he, the Lord, being "a priest for ever after the order of Melchizedek" [Ps. 110:4] and the anointed son of God from before the foundation of the world, and they, the begotten sons of Jesus through the gospel.[24]

---

[21]Discourse of 10 March 1844, recorded by James Burgess; *WJS,* 333.

[22]Discourse of 10 March 1844, recorded by Wilford Woodruff; *WJS,* 328.

[23]Discourse of 5 January 1841, recorded by William Clayton; *WJS,* 59.

[24]*Times and Seasons,* 1 September 1842, 905.

Acts 10:1–6

No wonder the angel told good old Cornelius that he must send for Peter to learn how to be saved. Peter could baptize, and angels could not, so long as there were legal officers in the flesh holding the keys of the kingdom, or the authority of the priesthood.[25]

Acts 10:44–48

There is a difference between the Holy Ghost and the gift of the Holy Ghost. Cornelius received the Holy Ghost before he was baptized, which was the convincing power of God unto him of the truth of the gospel. But he could not receive the gift of the Holy Ghost until after he was baptized. And had he not taken this sign [or] ordinances upon him, the Holy Ghost, which convinced him of the truth of God, would have left him until he obeyed those ordinances and received the gift of the Holy Ghost by the laying on of hands, according to the order of God.[26]

Acts 13:46–48

After this chosen family had rejected Christ and his proposals, the heralds of salvation said to them, "Lo, we turn unto the Gentiles." And the Gentiles received the covenant and were grafted in from whence the chosen family were broken off. But the Gentiles have not continued in the goodness of God but have departed from the faith that was once delivered to the Saints, and have broken the covenant in which their fathers were established, and have become high-minded, and have not feared. Therefore, but few of them will be gathered with the chosen family.[27]

---

[25]*Times and Seasons,* 1 September 1842, 905.

[26]Discourse of 20 March 1842, recorded by Wilford Woodruff; *WJS,* 108.

[27]Letter to the editor, *American Revivalist and Rochester Observer,* from Kirtland, Ohio, 4 January 1833; *PWJS,* 271.

Acts 16:16–18

They detected the spirit. And although she spake favorably of them, Paul commanded the spirit to come out of her and saved themselves from the opprobrium that might have been heaped upon their heads through an affiance with her in the development of her wicked principles, which they certainly would have been charged with if they had not rebuked the evil spirit.[28]

Acts 19:1–6

Baptism was the essential point on which they could receive the gift of the Holy Ghost. It seems that some sectarian Jew had been baptizing like John but had forgotten to inform them that there was one to follow by the name of Jesus Christ, to baptize with fire and the Holy Ghost, which showed these converts that their first baptism was illegal. And when they heard this, they were gladly baptized, and after hands were laid on them they received the gifts, according to promise, and spake with tongues and prophesied.[29]

"Not so, not so, my friends. If you had, you would have heard of the Holy Ghost. But you have been duped by some designing knave who has come in the name of John—an imposter." How do you know it, Paul? "Why John verily baptized with water unto repentance, always telling the people that they should believe on him that should come after him. He would baptize with fire and with the Holy Ghost." John's baptism stood good, but these had been baptized by some imposter.[30]

"No, John did not baptize you, for he did his work right." And so Paul went and baptized them, for he knew what the true doctrine was, and he knew that John had not baptized them.[31]

---

[28]*Times and Seasons,* 1 April 1842, 745.

[29]*Times and Seasons,* 1 September 1842, 904.

[30]Discourse of 10 March 1844, recorded by James Burgess; *WJS,* 333.

[31]Discourse of 10 March 1844, recorded by Wilford Woodruff; *WJS,* 328.

Acts 19:13–16

It is very evident that [evil spirits] possess a power that none but those who have the priesthood can control, as in the case of the sons of Sceva.[32]

Acts 20:28–30

Paul said to the elders of the church at Ephesus, after he had labored three years with them, that he knew that some of their own number would turn away from the faith and seek to lead away disciples after them. . . . After his departure from the church at Ephesus, many, even of the elders, turned away from the truth and, what is almost always the case, sought to lead away disciples after them. Strange as it may appear at first thought, yet it is no less so than true, that with all the professed determination to live godly, after turning from the faith of Christ, apostates have, unless they have speedily repented, sooner or later fallen into the snares of the wicked one and have been left destitute of the Spirit of God, to manifest their wickedness in the eyes of multitudes.[33]

Acts 26:1–29

[Paul] made his defense before King Agrippa, and related the account of the vision he had when he saw a light, and heard a voice; but still there were but few who believed him; some said he was dishonest, others said he was mad; and he was ridiculed and reviled. But all this did not destroy the reality of his vision. He had seen a vision, he knew he had, and all the persecution under heaven could not make it otherwise; and though they should persecute him unto death, yet he knew, and would know to his latest breath, that he had both seen a light and heard a voice

---

[32]*Times and Seasons,* 1 April 1842, 745.

[33]*Evening and Morning Star,* April 1834, 152.

speaking unto him, and all the world could not make him think or believe otherwise.[34]

Acts 27:22–24

The angel . . . came to Paul unobserved by the rest of the crew.[35]

---

[34]1839 History; *PJS,* 1:274; JS–H 1:24.

[35]*Times and Seasons,* 15 June 1842, 825.

Romans

Romans 1:16

Mormonism is the pure doctrine of Jesus Christ, of which I myself am not ashamed.[1]

Romans 2:12

[God] will judge them "not according to what they have not, but according to what they have" [2 Cor. 8:12]. Those who have lived without law will be judged without law, and those who have a law will be judged by that law. We need not doubt the wisdom and intelligence of the great Jehovah. He will award judgment or mercy to all nations according to their several deserts, their means of obtaining intelligence, the laws by which they are governed, the facilities afforded them of obtaining correct information, and his inscrutable designs in relation to the human family. And when the designs of God shall be made manifest and the curtain of futurity be withdrawn, we shall all of us eventually have to confess that the Judge of all the earth has done right. . . .

To say that the heathen would be damned because they did not believe the gospel would be preposterous. And to say that the Jews would all be damned that do not believe in Jesus would be equally absurd. For "how can they believe on him of whom they have not heard? And how can they hear without a preacher? And how can he preach except he be sent?" [Rom. 10:14–15]. Consequently, neither Jew nor heathen can be culpable for rejecting the conflicting opinions of sectarianism, nor for rejecting any testimony but that which is sent of God, for as the preacher cannot preach except he be sent, so the hearer cannot believe [except] he hear a sent preacher. And [he] cannot be condemned

---

[1]Letter to James A. Bennet, from Nauvoo, Illinois, 8 September 1842; *PJS,* 2:462.

for what he has not heard, and being without law [he] will have to be judged without law.[2]

Romans 8:16–17

We believe that God condescended to speak from the heavens and declare his will concerning the human family, give to them just and holy laws to regulate their conduct, and guide them in a direct way, that in due time he might take them to himself and make them joint heirs with his Son.[3]

No man can attain to the joint heirship with Jesus Christ without being administered to by one having the same power and authority of Melchizedek.[4]

To become a joint heir of the heirship of the Son, [one] must put away all [one's] traditions.[5]

[It is] to inherit the same power [and] exaltation, until you ascend the throne of eternal power, same as those who are gone before.[6]

What is it? To inherit the same glory, power, and exaltation, with those who are gone before.[7]

[You will] enjoy the same rise, exaltation, and glory, until you arrive at the station of a God.[8]

They are exalted far above principalities, thrones, dominions,

---

[2]*Times and Seasons,* 15 April 1842, 759-60.

[3]*Evening and Morning Star,* February 1834, 136.

[4]Discourse of 27 August 1843, recorded by Franklin D. Richards; *WJS,* 245.

[5]Discourse of 27 August 1843, recorded by Willard Richards; *WJS,* 244.

[6]Discourse of 7 April 1844, recorded by Thomas Bullock; *KFD,* 33.

[7]Discourse of 7 April 1844, recorded by William Clayton; *KFD,* 32.

[8]Discourse of 7 April 1844, recorded by Wilford Woodruff; *KFD,* 32.

and angels, and are expressly declared to be heirs of God and joint heirs with Jesus Christ, all having eternal power.[9]

The scripture says those who will obey the commandments shall be heirs of God and joint heirs with Jesus Christ.[10]

Romans 8:20

"The creature was made subject to vanity, not willingly, but Christ subjected the same in hope." We are all subject to vanity while we travel through the crooked paths and difficulties which surround us. Where is the man that is free from vanity? None ever were perfect but Jesus, and why was he perfect? Because he was the Son of God and had the fulness of the Spirit and greater power than any man. But notwithstanding our vanity, we look forward with hope (because "we are subjected in hope") to the time of our deliverance.[11]

Romans 9

All election that can be found in the scripture is according to the flesh and pertaining to the priesthood.[12]

The election there spoken of is pertaining to the flesh and has reference to the seed of Abraham, according to the promise God made to Abraham, saying, "In thee and in thy seed all the families of the earth shall be blessed" [Gen. 12:3]. To them belong the adoption and the covenants. ... The election of the promised seed still continues, and in the last days they shall have the priesthood restored unto them, and they shall be the "saviors on mount Zion," the "ministers of our God." ...

---

[9]Discourse of 16 June 1844, recorded by Thomas Bullock; *WJS*, 381.

[10]Discourse of 16 June 1844, recorded by George Laub; *WJS*, 382.

[11]Discourse of 16 May 1841, reported in *Times and Seasons*, 1 June 1841, 429.

[12]Discourse of 16 May 1841, recorded by William Clayton; *WJS*, 74.

The whole of the chapter had reference to the priesthood and the house of Israel. Unconditional election of individuals to eternal life was not taught by the apostles. God did elect or predestinate that all those who would be saved should be saved in Christ Jesus, and through obedience to the gospel. But he passes over no man's sins but visits them with correction, and if his children will not repent of their sins, he will discard them.[13]

Romans 10:14–15

And I will ask, how can they be sent without a revelation or some other visible display of the manifestation of God?[14]

Romans 10:17

Faith comes by hearing the word of God through the testimony of the servants of God. That testimony is always attended by the Spirit of prophecy and revelation. . . . Faith comes not by signs but by hearing the word of God.[15]

God may correct the scripture by me if he chooses: "Faith comes by hearing the word of God," and not "faith cometh by hearing, and hearing by the word of God."[16]

Truth carries its own influence and recommends itself.[17]

Every word that proceedeth from the mouth of Jehovah has such an influence over the human mind, the logical mind, that it

---

[13]Discourse of 16 May 1841, reported in *Times and Seasons,* 1 June 1841, 430.

[14]Letter to Isaac Galland, from Liberty Jail, Missouri, 22 March 1839; *Times and Seasons,* February 1840, 54.

[15]Discourse of 27 June 1839, recorded in Willard Richards's "Pocket Companion"; *WJS,* 3-4.

[16]Discourse of 13 April 1843, recorded by Willard Richards; *WJS,* 191.

[17]Discourse of 6 August 1843, recorded by Levi Richards; *WJS,* 237.

is convincing without other testimony. Faith cometh by hearing. If ten thousand men testify to a truth you know, would it add to your faith? No. Or will one thousand testimonies destroy your knowledge of a fact? No.[18]

Romans 12:19

There is a difference between the vengeance that belongeth to the Lord, and a man defending himself or [a] friend.[19]

---

[18]Discourse of 6 August 1843, recorded by Willard Richards; *WJS,* 237.

[19]Discourse of 2 March 1841, recorded by William P. McIntire; *WJS,* 64.

1 Corinthians

1 Corinthians 1:21

As Paul said, "the world by wisdom know not God," so the world by speculation are destitute of revelation.[1]

1 Corinthians 2:11, JST (2:10–14)

We shall finally have to come to the same conclusion that Paul did, that "no man knows the things of God but by the Spirit of God."[2]

We never can comprehend the things of God and of heaven but by revelation. We may spiritualize and express opinions to all eternity, but that is no authority.[3]

1 Corinthians 8:5–6

If Joseph Smith says there are Gods many and Lords many, they cry, "Away with him, crucify him." Mankind verily say that the scripture is with them. Search the scriptures; they testify of things that apostates would blaspheme. Paul, if Joseph Smith is a blasphemer, you are. I say there are Gods many and Lords many, but to us only one, and we are to be subject to that one. . . .

Some say, "I do not interpret [the] same as you." They say it means the heathen god. Paul says, "there are gods many." It makes a plurality of Gods anyhow. Without a revelation, I am not going to give the God of heaven to them anyhow. You know, and I testify, that Paul had no allusions to it. I have it from God, get over it if you can. I have a witness of the Holy Ghost and a testimony that Paul had no allusion to the heathen god in the text.[4]

See also under Revelation 1:6.

---

[1]*Times and Seasons,* 15 May 1843, 194.

[2]*Times and Seasons,* 15 June 1842, 825.

[3]Discourse of 8 April 1843, recorded by William Clayton; *WJS,* 186.

[4]Discourse of 16 June 1844, recorded by Thomas Bullock; *WJS,* 378–79.

1 Corinthians 10:1–4

Paul told about Moses' proceedings. [He] spoke of the children of Israel being baptized, and so forth. He knew this and that all the ordinances and blessings were in the Church.[5]

1 Corinthians 12:1

It is evident from this that some of them were ignorant in relation to these matters, or they would not need instruction.[6]

1 Corinthians 12:3

The passage which reads "No man can say that Jesus is the Lord, but by the Holy Ghost" should be translated "No man can *know* that Jesus is the Lord, but by the Holy Ghost."[7]

We believe that "no man can know that Jesus is the Christ, but by the Holy Ghost."[8]

1 Corinthians 12:4–11

We believe that we have a right to revelations, visions, and dreams from God, our Heavenly Father, and light and intelligence through the gift of the Holy Ghost, in the name of Jesus Christ, on all subjects pertaining to our spiritual welfare, if it so be that we keep his commandments so as to render ourselves worthy in his sight.[9]

---

[5]Discourse of summer of 1839, recorded in Willard Richards's "Pocket Companion"; *WJS*, 10.

[6]*Times and Seasons,* 15 June 1842, 824.

[7]Discourse of 28 April 1842, recorded by Eliza R. Snow; *WJS*, 115.

[8]*Times and Seasons,* 15 June 1842, 823.

[9]Letter to Isaac Galland, from Liberty Jail, Missouri, 22 March 1839; *Times and Seasons,* February 1840, 54.

We believe in the gift of tongues, prophecy, revelation, visions, healing, interpretation of tongues, and so forth.[10]

It not infrequently occurs that when the elders of this Church preach to the inhabitants of the world that if they obey the gospel they shall receive the gift of the Holy Ghost, that the people expect to see some wonderful manifestation, some great display of power, or some extraordinary miracle performed. And it is often the case that young members in this Church, for want of better information, carry along with them their old notions of things and sometimes fall into egregious errors. . . .

We believe in the gift of the Holy Ghost being enjoyed now as much as it was in the apostles' days. We believe that it is necessary to make and to organize the priesthood, [and] that no man can be called to fill any office in the ministry without it. We also believe in prophecy, in tongues, in visions, and in revelations, in gifts, and in healings, and that these things cannot be enjoyed without the gift of the Holy Ghost. . . . We believe in it in all its fullness, and power, and greatness, and glory. But whilst we do this, we believe in it rationally, reasonably, consistently, and scripturally, and not according to the wild vagaries, foolish notions, and traditions of men.

The human family are very apt to run to extremes, especially in religious matters. And hence people in general either want some miraculous display, or they will not believe in the gift of the Holy Ghost at all. If an elder lays his hands upon a person, it is thought by many that the person must immediately rise and speak in tongues and prophesy. . . . We believe that the Holy Ghost is imparted by the laying on of hands of those in authority, and that the gift of tongues and also the gift of prophecy are gifts of the Spirit and are obtained through that medium. But then to say that men always prophesied and spoke in tongues when they had the imposition of hands would be to state that which is

---

[10]*Times and Seasons,* 1 March 1842, 709; A of F 7.

untrue, contrary to the practice of the apostles, and at variance with holy writ. For Paul says, "To one is given the gift of tongues, to another the gift of prophecy, and to another the gift of healing." And again, "Do all prophesy? Do all speak with tongues? Do all interpret?" [1 Cor. 12:29–30], evidently showing that all did not possess these several gifts, but that one received one gift, and another received another gift. All did not prophesy, all did not speak in tongues, all did not work miracles, but all did receive the gift of the Holy Ghost. Sometimes they spake in tongues and prophesied in the apostles' days, and sometimes they did not. The same is the case with us also in our administrations, while more frequently there is no manifestation at all that is visible to the surrounding multitude. . . . All the gifts of the Spirit are not visible to the natural vision or understanding of man. Indeed, very few of them are. . . .

These, then, are all gifts. They come from God, they are of God, they are all the gifts of the Holy Ghost. They are what Christ ascended into heaven to impart, and yet how few of them could be known by the generality of men. . . . Paul says, "There are diversities of gifts, yet the same Spirit. . . . But all these worketh that one and the selfsame Spirit, dividing to each man severally as he will." There are several gifts mentioned here, yet which of them all could be known by an observer at the imposition of hands? The word of wisdom and the word of knowledge are as much gifts as any other, yet if a person possessed both of these gifts, or received them by the imposition of hands, who would know it? Another might receive the gift of faith, and they would be as ignorant of it. Or suppose a man had the gift of healing, or power to work miracles. That would not then be known. It would require time and circumstances to call these gifts into operation. Suppose a man had the discerning of spirits. Who would be the wiser for it? . . . The greatest, the best, and the most useful gifts would be known nothing about by an observer. . . .

The manifestations of the gift of the Holy Ghost, the ministering of angels, or the development of the power, majesty, or glory of God, were very seldom manifested publicly, and that generally to the people of God, as to the Israelites. But most generally, when angels have come or God has revealed himself, it has been to individuals in private, in their chamber, in the wilderness or fields, and that generally without noise or tumult. . . . The Lord cannot always be known by the thunder of his voice, by the display of his glory, or by the manifestation of his power. And those that are the most anxious to see these things are the least prepared to meet them. And were the Lord to manifest his powers as he did to the children of Israel, such characters would be the first to say, "Let not the Lord speak any more, lest we his people die" [Ex. 20:19].

We would say to the brethren, seek to know God in your closets, call upon him in the fields. Follow the directions of the Book of Mormon and pray over, and for, your families, your cattle, your flocks, your herds, your corn, and all things that you possess [Alma 34:20–25]. Ask the blessing of God upon all your labors and everything that you engage in. Be virtuous and pure. Be men of integrity and truth. Keep the commandments of God, and then you will be able more perfectly to understand the difference between right and wrong, between the things of God and the things of men. And your path will be like that of the just, "which shineth brighter and brighter unto the perfect day" [Prov. 4:18]. . . .

The gifts of God are all useful in their place, but when they are applied to that which God does not intend, they prove an injury, a snare, and a curse, instead of a blessing.[11]

[In answer to the question, "May I not repent and be baptized and not pay any attention to dreams and visions?"]:

Suppose I am traveling and I am hungry and meet a man and tell him I am hungry. He tells me to go yonder: "There is a house for entertainment. Go knock, and you must conform to all the rules of the house or you cannot satisfy your hunger. Knock, call for food, and sit down and eat." And I go and knock and ask for

---

[11]*Times and Seasons,* 15 June 1842, 823–26.

food and sit down to the table but do not eat. Shall I satisfy my hunger? No, I must eat. The gifts [of the Spirit] are the food. The graces of the Spirit are the gifts of the Spirit.[12]

1 Corinthians 12:10

The gift of discerning spirits will be given to the presiding elder. Pray for him, that he may have this gift.[13]

1 Corinthians 12:14–30

[It is] the disposition of man to consider the lower offices in the Church dishonorable and to look with jealous eyes upon the standing of others. It is the nonsense of the human heart for a person to be aspiring to other stations than [those] appointed of God. It is better for individuals to magnify their respective callings and wait patiently till God shall say to them, "Come up higher."[14]

The advancement of the cause of God and the building up of Zion is as much one man's business as another's. The only difference is that one is called to fulfill one duty and another another duty. But if one member suffers, all the members suffer with it, and if one member is honored, all the rest rejoice with it. And the eye cannot say to the ear, "I have no need of thee," nor the head to the foot, "I have no need of thee." Party feelings, separate interests, and exclusive designs should be lost sight of in the one common cause, in the interest of the whole.[15]

The Church is a compact body composed of different members and is strictly analogous to the human system. And Paul,

---

[12]Statement of 2 January 1843, recorded by Willard Richards; *PJS*, 3.

[13]Discourse of summer of 1839, recorded in Willard Richards's "Pocket Companion"; *WJS*, 12.

[14]Discourse of 28 April 1842, recorded by Eliza R. Snow; *WJS*, 115.

[15]*Times and Seasons*, 2 May 1842, 776.

after speaking of the different gifts, says, "Now ye are the body of Christ, and each one a member in particular. . . . Are all apostles? Are all prophets? Are all teachers? Are all workers of miracles? Have all the gifts of healing? Do all speak with tongues? Do all interpret?" It is evident that they do not. Yet are they all members of the one body? All members of the natural body? Are not the eye, the ear, the head, or the hand? Yet the eye cannot say to the ear, "I have no need of thee," nor the head to the foot, "I have no need of thee." They are all so many component parts in the perfect machine, the one body. And if one member suffers, the whole of the members suffer with it. And if one member rejoices, all the rest are honored with it.[16]

See also under 1 Corinthians 12:4–11.

1 Corinthians 13:1

Don't be limited in your views with regard to your neighbors' virtues, but be limited toward your own virtues, and not think yourselves more righteous than others. You must enlarge your souls toward others if you would do like Jesus and carry your fellow creatures to Abraham's bosom.[17]

1 Corinthians 14:1

It is very evident from these scriptures that many of them had not spiritual gifts, for if they had spiritual gifts, where was the necessity of Paul telling them to follow after them?[18]

1 Corinthians 14:2–33

Tongues were given for the purpose of preaching among those whose language is not understood, as on the day of

---

[16]*Times and Seasons,* 15 June 1842, 824.

[17]Discourse of 28 April 1842, recorded by Eliza R. Snow; *WJS,* 118.

[18]*Times and Seasons,* 15 June 1842, 824.

Pentecost [Acts 2:4–12]. It is not necessary for tongues to be taught to the Church particularly, for any man that has the Holy Ghost can speak of the things of God in his own tongue, as well as to speak in another.[19]

Speak not in the gift of tongues without understanding it or without interpretation. The Devil can speak in tongues. The Adversary will come with his work; he can tempt all classes [and] can speak in English or Dutch. Let no one speak in tongues unless he interprets, except by the consent of the one who is placed to preside. Then he may discern or interpret, or another may.[20]

The gift of tongues is necessary in the Church. If Satan could not speak in tongues, he could not tempt a Dutchman, or any other nation but the English, for he can tempt the Englishman for he has tempted me, and I am an Englishman. But the gift of tongues, by the power of the Holy Ghost in the Church, is for the benefit of the servants of God to preach to unbelievers, as on the day of Pentecost. When devout men from every nation shall assemble to hear the things of God, let the elders preach to them in their own mother tongue, whether it is German, French, Spanish, Irish, or any other. And let those interpret who understand the languages spoken, in their own mother tongue.[21]

If any have a matter to reveal, let it be in your own tongue. Do not indulge too much in the gift of tongues, or the Devil will take advantage of the innocent. You may speak in tongues for your own comfort, but I lay this down for a rule, that if anything

---

[19]Discourse of 27 June 1839, recorded in Willard Richards's "Pocket Companion"; *WJS*, 3–4.

[20]Discourse of summer of 1839, recorded in Willard Richards's "Pocket Companion"; *WJS*, 12.

[21]Discourse of 26 December 1841, recorded by Willard Richards; *PJS*, 2:345.

is taught by the gift of tongues, it is not to be received for doctrine.[22]

There are only two gifts that could be made visible—the gift of tongues and the gift of prophecy. These are things that are the most talked about, and yet if a person spoke in an unknown tongue, according to Paul's testimony, he would be a "barbarian" to those present. They would say that it was gibberish. And if he prophesied, they would call it nonsense. The gift of tongues is the smallest gift perhaps of the whole, and yet it is one that is the most sought after. . . . Be not so curious about tongues. Do not speak in tongues except there be an interpreter present. The ultimate design of tongues is to speak to foreigners, and if persons are very anxious to display their intelligence, let them speak to such in their own tongues.[23]

See also under 1 Corinthians 12:4–11.

1 Corinthians 15:3–4

The fundamental principles of our religion are the testimony of the apostles and prophets concerning Jesus Christ, that he died, was buried, rose again the third day, and ascended up into heaven. And all other things are only appendages to these, which pertain to our religion.[24]

1 Corinthians 15:12–20

If the resurrection from the dead is not an important point or item in our faith, we must confess that we know nothing about it. For if there is no resurrection from the dead, then Christ has not risen. And if Christ has not risen, he was not the Son of God. And if he was not the Son of God, there is not nor cannot be a Son of

---

[22]Discourse of 28 April 1842, recorded by Eliza R. Snow; *WJS,* 119.

[23]*Times and Seasons,* 15 June 1842, 825.

[24]*Elders' Journal,* July 1838, 44.

God if the present book called the scriptures is true. . . . If he has risen from the dead, he will by his power bring all men to stand before him. For if he has risen from the dead, the bands of the temporal death are broken that the grave has no victory [1 Cor. 15:54–55]. If, then, the grave has no victory, those who keep the sayings of Jesus and obey his teachings have not only a promise of a resurrection from the dead, but an assurance of being admitted into his glorious kingdom. For he himself says, "Where I am, there shall also my servant be" [John 12:26].[25]

I will tell you what I want, if tomorrow I shall be called to lay in yonder tomb. In the morning of the resurrection, let me strike hands with my father and cry, "My father!" And he will say, "My son, my son!," as soon as the rock rends and before we come out of our graves. . . .

Would you think it strange that I relate what I have seen in vision in relation [to] this interesting theme? Those who have died in Jesus Christ may expect to enter into all that fruition of joy, when they come forth, which they have pursued here. So plain was the vision. I actually saw men, before they had ascended from the tomb, as though they were getting up slowly. They took each other by the hand, and it was "My father!" and "My son!" "My mother!" and "My daughter!" "My brother!" and "My sister!" When the voice calls, suppose I am laid by the side of my father. What would be the first joy of my heart? Where is my father? My mother? My sister? They are by my side. I embrace them and they me.

It is my meditation all the day, and more than my meat and drink, to know how I shall make the Saints of God to comprehend the visions that roll like an overflowing surge before my mind. Oh how I would delight to bring before you things which you never thought of, but poverty and the cares of the world prevent. But I am glad I have the privilege of communicating to you

---

[25]*Evening and Morning Star,* March 1834, 144.

some things, which, if grasped closely, will be a help to you when the clouds are gathering and the storms are ready to burst upon you like peals of thunder. Lay hold of these things and let not your knees tremble, nor your hearts faint. What can earthquakes, wars, and tornados do? Nothing. All your losses will be made up to you in the resurrection, provided you continue faithful. By the vision of the Almighty, I have seen it. More painful to me [is] the thought of annihilation than death. If I had no expectation of seeing my mother, brothers and sisters, and friends again, my heart would burst in a moment and I should go down to my grave. The expectation of seeing my friends in the morning of the resurrection cheers my soul and makes me bear up against the evils of life. It is like their taking a long journey, and on their return we meet them with increased joy.

God has revealed his Son from the heavens and the doctrine of the resurrection also. And we have a knowledge that these we bury here, God brings them up again, clothed upon and quickened by the spirit of the great God.[26]

1 Corinthians 15:21–22

All shall be raised from the dead. The Lamb of God hath brought to pass the resurrection so that all shall rise from the dead.[27]

1 Corinthians 15:29

Aside from my knowledge independent of the Bible, I would say that [baptism for the dead] was certainly practiced by the ancient churches, and St. Paul endeavors to prove the doctrine of the resurrection from the same. . . . The Saints have the privilege of being baptized for those of their relatives who are dead, who

---

[26]Discourse of 16 April 1843, recorded by Willard Richards; *WJS*, 195–96.

[27]Discourse of 12 May 1844, recorded by Thomas Bullock; *WJS*, 368.

they feel to believe would have embraced the gospel if they had been privileged with hearing it, and who have received the gospel in the spirit through the instrumentality of those who may have been commissioned to preach to them while in prison. . . . You will undoubtedly see its consistency and reasonableness. [It] presents the gospel of Christ in probably a more enlarged scale than some have viewed it.[28]

The Bible supports the doctrine [of baptism for the dead]. If there is one word of the Lord that supports the doctrine, it is enough to make it a true doctrine. Again, if we can baptize a man in the name of the Father, [and] of the Son, and of the Holy Ghost for the remission of sins, it is just as much our privilege to act as an agent and be baptized for the remission of sins for and in behalf of our dead kindred who have not heard the gospel or fulness of it.[29]

See also under 1 Peter 3:18–19; 4:6.

1 Corinthians 15:42–44
See under 1 Corinthians 15:50–53.

1 Corinthians 15:50–53
Flesh and blood cannot go there, but flesh and bones, quickened by the Spirit of God, can.[30]

Flesh and blood cannot inherit the kingdom of God, or the kingdom that God inherits or inhabits, but the flesh without the blood, and the Spirit of God flowing in the veins instead of the blood. For blood is the part of the body that causes corruption. Therefore, we

---

[28]Letter to the Twelve in Britain, from Nauvoo, Illinois, 15 December 1840; *PWJS*, 486.

[29]Discourse of 27 March 1842, recorded by Wilford Woodruff; *WJS*, 109–10.

[30]Discourse of 9 October 1843, recorded by Willard Richards; *WJS*, 255.

must be changed in the twinkle of an eye, or have to lay down these tabernacles and [let] the blood vanish away. Therefore, Jesus Christ left his blood to atone for the sins of the world, that he might ascend into the presence of the Father. . . . The blood is the corruptible part of the tabernacles. The resurrection is devised to take away corruption and make man perfect, or in the glory [in] which he was created. For the body is sown in corruption and raised in incorruption. Then we will be able to go into the presence of God.[31]

See also under Isaiah 33:14.

---

[31]Discourse of 12 May 1844, recorded by George Laub; *WJS,* 370–71.

2 Corinthians

2 Corinthians 5:10, JST

[God] holds the reins of judgment in his hands. He is a wise lawgiver and will judge all men, not according to the narrow contracted notions of men, but "according to the deeds done in the body, whether they be good or evil," or whether these deeds were done in England, America, Spain, Turkey, or India.[1]

2 Corinthians 11:16–31

As Paul boasted, I have suffered more than Paul did. I should be like a fish out of water if I were out of persecutions. Perhaps my brethren think it requires all this to keep me humble. The Lord has constituted me so curiously that I glory in persecution. I am not nearly so humble as if I were not persecuted.[2]

2 Corinthians 12:1–4

Paul had seen the third heavens, and I more.[3]

There are some things in my own bosom that must remain there. If Paul could say, "I knew a man who ascended to the third heaven and saw things unlawful for man to utter," I more.[4]

---

[1]*Times and Seasons,* 15 April 1842, 759.

[2]Discourse of 26 May 1844, recorded by Thomas Bullock; *WJS,* 373.

[3]Discourse of 17 May 1843; recorded by William Clayton; *WJS,* 202.

[4]Discourse of 21 May 1843, recorded by Martha Jane Coray; *WJS,* 207.

Galatians

Galatians 1:6–9

Beware of all disaffected characters, for they come not to build up, but to destroy and scatter abroad. Though we or an angel from heaven preach any other gospel or introduce [any] order of things [other] than those things which ye have received and are authorized to receive from the First Presidency, let him be accursed.[1]

If any man preach any other gospel with that which I have preached, he shall be cursed.[2]

Galatians 2:11–14

Paul [was] contending with Peter face to face, with sound and irresistible arguments.[3]

Galatians 3:8

It will be noticed that according to Paul, the gospel was preached to Abraham. We would like to be informed in what name the gospel was then preached, whether it was in the name of Christ or some other name. If in any other name, was it the gospel? And if it was the gospel, and that preached in the name of Christ, had it any ordinances? If not, was it the gospel? And if it had, what were they? Our friends may say, perhaps, that there were never any ordinances except those of offering sacrifices, before the coming of Christ, and that it could not be possible for

---

[1]Letter to the Brethren, n.d. [1837]; *PJS,* 2:220.

[2]Discourse of 12 May 1844, recorded by Thomas Bullock; *WJS,* 368.

[3]Letter to William Smith, from Kirtland, Ohio, 18 December 1835; *PJS,* 2:117. The phrase "and irresistible" is added from the copy in the 1834–36 History; *PJS,* 1:173.

the gospel to have been administered while the sacrifices of blood were. But we will recollect that Abraham offered sacrifice and notwithstanding this had the gospel preached to him. That the offering of sacrifice was only to point the mind forward to Christ we infer from these remarkable words of his to the Jews: "Your father Abraham rejoiced to see my day: and he saw it, and was glad" [John 8:56]. So, then, because the ancients offered sacrifice it did not hinder their hearing the gospel but served, as we said before, to open their eyes and enable them to look forward to the time of the coming of the Savior, and to rejoice in his redemption.[4]

Galatians 3:19

It is said in Gal. 3:19 that the law of Moses, or the Levitical law, was "added" because of transgression. What, we ask, was this law added to, if it was not added to the gospel? It must be plain that it was added to the gospel, since we learn that they had the gospel preached to them [Heb. 4:2].[5]

Offerings, sacrifices, and carnal commandments were added in consequence of transgression. And they that did them should live by them [Gal. 3:12].[6]

---

[4]*Evening and Morning Star,* March 1834, 143.

[5]*Evening and Morning Star,* March 1834, 143.

[6]Discourse of 27 August 1843, recorded by James Burgess; *WJS,* 246.

Ephesians

Ephesians 1:9–10

The work of the Lord in these last days is one of vast magnitude and almost beyond the comprehension of mortals. Its glories are past description and its grandeur unsurpassable. It has been the theme which has animated the bosom of prophets and righteous men from the creation of this world down through every succeeding generation to the present time. And it is truly the dispensation of the fulness of times, when all things which are in Christ Jesus, whether in heaven or on the earth, shall be gathered together in him, and when all things shall be restored, as spoken of by all the holy prophets since the world began. For in it will take place the glorious fulfillment of the promises made to the fathers, while the displays of the power of the Most High will be great, glorious, and sublime. . . .

Here, then, beloved brethren, is a work to engage in worthy of archangels—a work which will cast into the shade the things which have heretofore been accomplished, a work which kings and prophets and righteous men in former ages have sought, expected, and earnestly desired to see, but died without the sight. And well will it be for those who shall aid in carrying into effect the mighty operations of Jehovah.[1]

Now the "purpose in himself" in the winding up scene of the last dispensation is that all things pertaining to that dispensation should be conducted precisely in accordance with the preceding dispensations. And again, God purposed in himself that there should not be an eternal fulness until every dispensation should be fulfilled and gathered together in one, and that all things whatsoever that should be gathered together in one in those dispensations, unto the same fulness and eternal glory, should be in Christ Jesus. Therefore, he set the ordinances to be the same for ever

---

[1]*Times and Seasons,* October 1840, 178–79.

175

and ever and set Adam to watch over them, to reveal them from heaven to man or to send angels to reveal them. . . .

Paul perfectly understood the purpose of God in relation to his connection with man, and that glorious and perfect order which he established in himself whereby he sent forth power, revelations, and glory.[2]

The dispensation of the fulness of times will bring to light the things that have been revealed in all former dispensations, also other things that have not been before revealed.[3]

Truly, this is a day long to be remembered by the Saints of the last days, a day in which the God of heaven has begun to restore the ancient order of his kingdom unto his servants and his people, a day in which all things are concurring together to bring about the completion of the fulness of the gospel, a fulness of the dispensation of dispensations, even the fulness of times, a day in which God has begun to make manifest and set in order in his Church those things which have been, and those things which the ancient prophets and wise men desired to see but died without beholding it, a day in which those things begin to be made manifest which have been hid from before the foundations of the world, and which Jehovah has promised should be made known in his own due time unto his servants, to prepare the earth for the return of his glory, even a celestial glory, and a kingdom of priests and kings to God and the Lamb forever, on Mount Zion, or the hundred and forty and four thousand whom John the Revelator saw, which should come to pass in the restitution of all things.[4]

---

[2]Discourse of 5 October 1840, recorded by Robert B. Thompson; *WJS,* 39–40.

[3]Discourse of 3 October 1841, recorded in *Times and Seasons,* 15 October 1841, 578.

[4]Journal, 6 January 1842; *PJS,* 2:352.

The building up of Zion is a cause that has interested the people of God in every age. It is a theme upon which prophets, priests, and kings have dwelt with peculiar delight. They have looked forward with joyful anticipation to the day in which we live, and fired with heavenly and joyful anticipations they have sung, and written, and prophesied of this our day. But they died without the sight. We are the favored people that God has made choice of to bring about the latter-day glory. It is left for us to see, participate in, and help to roll forward the latter-day glory, "the dispensation of the fulness of times," when God will "gather together all things that are in heaven, and all things that are upon the earth, even in one," when the Saints of God will be gathered in, one from every nation, and kindred, and people, and tongue, when the Jews will be gathered together into one, and the wicked will also be gathered together to be destroyed, as spoken of by the prophets. The Spirit of God will also dwell with his people and be withdrawn from the rest of the nations. And all things, whether in heaven or on earth, will be in one, even in Christ.

The heavenly priesthood will unite with the earthly to bring about those great purposes. And whilst we are thus united in the one common cause to roll forth the kingdom of God, the heavenly priesthood are not idle spectators. The Spirit of God will be showered down from above; it will dwell in our midst. The blessings of the Most High will rest upon our tabernacles, and our name will be handed down to future ages. Our children will rise up and call us blessed, and generations yet unborn will dwell with peculiar delight upon the scenes that we have passed through, the privations that we have endured, the untiring zeal that we have manifested, the insurmountable difficulties that we have overcome in laying the foundation of a work that brought about the glory and blessings which they will realize, a work that God and angels have contemplated with delight for generations past, that fired the souls of the ancient patriarchs and prophets, a work that is destined to bring about the destruction of the powers of darkness, the renovation of the earth, the glory of God, and the salvation of the human family.[5]

It is necessary in the ushering in of the dispensation of the fulness of times, which dispensation is now beginning to usher in, that a whole and complete and perfect union, and welding together of dispensations, and keys, and powers, and glories should take place, and be revealed from the days of Adam even to the present time. And not only this, but those things which never have been revealed from the foundation of the world, but have been kept hid from the wise and prudent, shall be revealed unto babes and sucklings in this, the dispensation of the fulness of times.

Now, what do we hear in the gospel which we have received? A voice of gladness! A voice of mercy from heaven; and a voice of truth out of the earth. . . . The voice of Peter, James, and John in the wilderness between Harmony, Susquehanna county, and Colesville, Broome county, on the Susquehanna river, declaring themselves as possessing the keys of the kingdom, and of the dispensation of the fulness of times! . . . And the voice of Michael, the archangel; the voice of Gabriel, and of Raphael, and of divers angels, from Michael or Adam down to the present time, all declaring their dispensation, their rights, their keys, their honors, their majesty and glory, and the power of their priesthood; giving line upon line, precept upon precept; here a little, and there a little; giving us consolation by holding forth that which is to come, confirming our hope![6]

Ephesians 2:20

The only difference between [sectarian] religion and mine is that I firmly believe in the prophets and apostles, Jesus Christ

---

[5]*Times and Seasons,* 2 May 1842, 776.

[6]*Times and Seasons,* 1 October 1842, 935–36; D&C 128:18–21.

being the chief corner stone, and speak as one having authority among them, and not as the scribes.[7]

Ephesians 4:4–6

The cause of God is one common cause, in which all the Saints are alike interested. We are all members of the one common body, and all partake of the same spirit, and are baptized into one baptism, and possess alike the same glorious hope.[8]

Ephesians 4:11

And how were apostles, prophets, pastors, teachers, and evangelists chosen? By prophecy (revelation) and by laying on of hands. By a divine communication and a divinely appointed ordinance, through the medium of the priesthood, organized according to the order of God by divine appointment.[9]

Ephesians 5:22–33

See under 1 Peter 3:1, 5–7.

Ephesians 6:5–9

The servant . . . is commanded to be in obedience, as unto the Lord. The master in turn is required to treat them with kindness before God, understanding at the same time that he is to give an account.[10]

Ephesians 6:11–13

Let us be wise in all things and keep all the commandments

---

[7]Letter to Isaac Galland, from Liberty Jail, Missouri, 22 March 1839; *Times and Seasons*, February 1840, 52–53.

[8]*Times and Seasons*, 2 May 1842, 776.

[9]*Times and Seasons*, 1 April 1842, 744–45.

[10]*Messenger and Advocate*, April 1836, 291.

of God, that our salvation may be sure. Having our armor ready and prepared against the time appointed, and having on the whole armor of righteousness, we may be able to stand in that trying day.[11]

---

[11]Letter to Hezekiah Peck, from Kirtland, Ohio, 31 August 1835; *PWJS*, 347.

Philippians

Philippians 4:8

We believe in being honest, true, chaste, benevolent, virtuous, and in doing good to all men; indeed, we may say that we follow the admonition of Paul—We believe all things, we hope all things, we have endured many things, and hope to be able to endure all things. If there is any thing virtuous, lovely, or of good report or praiseworthy, we seek after these things.[1]

------

[1] *Times and Seasons,* 1 March 1842, 710; A of F 13.

Colossians

Colossians 2:9
See under Hebrews 1:3.

1 Thessalonians

1 Thessalonians 4:7

Remember, brethren, that he has called you unto holiness and, need we say, to be like him in purity. How wise, how holy, how chaste, and how perfect, then, you ought to conduct yourselves in his sight.[1]

1 Thessalonians 4:13–18

Let us not sorrow as those without hope. The time is fast approaching when we shall see [our loved ones] again and rejoice together, without being afraid of wicked men. Yes, those who have slept in Christ shall he bring with him when he shall come to be glorified in his Saints and admired by all those who believe, but to take vengeance upon his enemies and all those who obey not the gospel. At that time, the hearts of the widow and fatherless shall be comforted, and every tear shall be wiped from off their faces.[2]

1 Thessalonians 5:1–6

We shall therefore do well to discern the signs of the times, as we pass along, that the day of the Lord may not overtake us "as a thief in the night."[3]

1 Thessalonians 5:2

The day of vengeance is coming upon this generation like a thief in the night; prejudice, blindness, and darkness fill the minds of many and cause them to persecute the true Church and reject the true light.[4]

---

[1]*Evening and Morning Star,* March 1834, 142.

[2]*Times and Seasons,* November 1839, 8.

[3]*Times and Seasons,* November 1839, 9.

[4]1839 History; *PJS,* 1:370.

2 Timothy

2 Timothy 3:1

We see that perilous times have truly come, and the things which we have so long expected have at last begun to usher in.[1]

2 Timothy 4:6–8

No one who believes the account will doubt for a moment this assertion of Paul which was made, as he knew, just before he was to take his leave of this world. Though he once, according to his own word, persecuted the Church of God and wasted it, yet after embracing the faith his labors were unceasing to spread the glorious news. And like a faithful soldier, when called to give his life in the cause which he had espoused, he laid it down, as he says, with an assurance of an eternal crown.

Follow the labors of this apostle from the time of his conversion to the time of his death, and you will have a fair sample of industry and patience in promulgating the gospel of Christ. Whipped, stoned, and derided, the moment he escaped the hands of his persecutors he as zealously as ever proclaimed the doctrine of the Savior. And all may know that he did not embrace the faith for the honor of this life, nor for the gain of earthly goods. What, then, could have induced him to undergo all this toil? It was, as he said, that he might obtain that crown of righteousness from the hand of God. No one, we presume, will doubt the faithfulness of Paul to the end. None will say that he did not keep the faith, that he did not fight the good fight, that he did not preach and persuade to the last. And what was he to receive? A crown of righteousness. And what shall others receive who do not labor faithfully and continue to the end? We leave such to search out

---

[1]Letter to Presendia Huntington Buell, from Liberty Jail, Missouri, 15 March 1839; *PWJS,* 387.

their own promises, if any they have. And if they have any they are welcome to them, on our part, for the Lord says that every man is to receive according to his works. Reflect for a moment, brethren, and enquire whether you would consider yourselves worthy [for] a seat at the marriage feast with Paul and others like him if you had been unfaithful. Had you not fought the good fight and kept the faith, could you expect to receive? Have you a promise of receiving a crown of righteousness from the hand of the Lord with the Church of the Firstborn? Here, then, we understand that Paul rested his hope in Christ, because he had kept the faith and loved his appearing; and from his hand he had a promise of receiving a crown of righteousness.[2]

---

[2]*Evening and Morning Star,* March 1834, 144.

Hebrews

Hebrews 1:3

Christ, who is the image of man, is also the express image of his Father's person. So says Paul. For in him, Christ, dwelt "the fulness of the Godhead bodily" [Col. 2:9]. Why? Because he was "the brightness of his glory, and the express image of his person." What person? God's person.[1]

Hebrews 1:14

These angels are under the direction of Michael or Adam, who acts under the direction of Christ.[2]

Hebrews 4:2

We find that when the Israelites came out of Egypt they had the gospel preached to them, according to Paul in his letter to the Hebrews.[3]

Hebrews 5:4

We believe that no man can administer salvation through the gospel to the souls of men in the name of Jesus Christ except he is authorized from God by revelation or by being ordained by someone whom God hath sent by revelation. . . . And I would ask, how was Aaron called, but by revelation?[4]

---

[1]Discourse of 9 July 1843, recorded by James Burgess; *WJS,* 231.

[2]Discourse of 5 October 1840, recorded by Robert B. Thompson; *WJS,* 39.

[3]*Evening and Morning Star,* March 1834, 143.

[4]Letter to Isaac Galland, from Liberty Jail, Missouri, 22 March 1839; *Times and Seasons,* February 1840, 54.

We believe that a man must be called of God, by prophecy, and by the laying on of hands by those who are in authority, to preach the Gospel and administer in the ordinances thereof.[5]

Aaron received his call by revelation.[6]

Hebrews 6:1–2

We shall commence with the first principles of the gospel, which are repentance and baptism for the remission of sins, and the gift of the Holy Ghost by the laying on of the hands. This we believe to be our duty, to teach to all mankind the doctrine of repentance.[7]

We believe in the doctrine of faith, and of repentance, and of baptism for the remission of sins, and the gift of the Holy Ghost by the laying on of hands, and of the resurrection of the dead, and of eternal judgment. . . . Now all these are the doctrines set forth by the apostles, and if we have anything to do with one of them, they are all alike precious and binding on us. . . . I consider these to be some of the leading items of the gospel as taught by Christ and his apostles, and as received by those whom they taught.[8]

Not laying again the doctrine of Christ, go on unto perfection. Obtain that Holy Spirit of Promise. Then you can be sealed to eternal life.[9]

---

[5] *Times and Seasons,* 1 March 1842, 709; A of F 5.

[6] Discourse of 22 January 1843, recorded by Wilford Woodruff; *WJS,* 157.

[7] *Messenger and Advocate,* September 1835, 180.

[8] Letter to Isaac Galland, from Liberty Jail, Missouri, 22 March 1839; *Times and Seasons,* February 1840, 54, 55.

[9] Discourse of summer of 1839, recorded in Willard Richards's "Pocket Companion"; *WJS,* 15.

The doctrine of eternal judgment was perfectly understood by the apostle, [as] is evident from several passages of scripture.[10]

We believe that through the Atonement of Christ, all mankind may be saved by obedience to the laws and ordinances of the gospel. We believe that these ordinances are, first, faith in the Lord Jesus Christ; second, repentance; third, baptism by immersion for the remission of sins; fourth, laying on of hands for the gift of the Holy Ghost.[11]

The first principles of the gospel, as I believe, [are] first, faith, repentance, baptism for the remission of sins, with the promise of the Holy Ghost.

Contradictions: "Leaving the principles of the doctrine of Christ." If a man leave the principles of the doctrine of Christ, how can he be saved in the principles? [It is] a contradiction; I don't believe it. I will render it therefore, *"Not* leaving the principles of the doctrine of Christ."[12]

I advise all to go on to perfection and search deeper and deeper into the mysteries of godliness.[13]

The doctrine of eternal judgments belongs to the first principles of the gospel in the last days.[14]

Hebrews 6:4–6

Now we come to talk about election. A great deal is said about it, one way or another. The Presbyterian says, once in

---

[10]Discourse of 16 May 1841, reported in *Times and Seasons,* 1 June 1841, 429.

[11]*Times and Seasons,* 1 March 1842, 709; see A of F 3 and 4.

[12]Discourse of 15 October 1843, recorded by Willard Richards; *WJS,* 256.

[13]Discourse of 12 May 1844, recorded by Thomas Bullock; *WJS,* 366.

[14]Discourse of 12 May 1844, recorded by Thomas Bullock; *WJS,* 367.

grace always in grace. The Methodist says, once in grace [one] can fall from grace and be renewed again. There is some truth in both of these statements. Paul says in the sixth chapter of Hebrews that after arriving at a certain knowledge and then falling away, it is impossible to renew them again. Well, Paul, the Presbyterian says, once in grace always in grace. I say it is not so. The Methodist says, once in grace [one] can fall from grace and be renewed again. "I, Paul, say it is impossible, seeing that they crucify to themselves the Son of God afresh, and put him to an open shame."[15]

Here is the doctrine of election that the world has quarreled so much about, but they do not know anything about it. The doctrine that the Presbyterians and Methodists have quarreled so much about—once in grace always in grace, or, falling away from grace—I will say a word about. They are both wrong. Truth takes a road between them both. For while the Presbyterian says once in grace you cannot fall, the Methodist says you can have grace today, fall from it tomorrow, next day have grace again, and so follow it. But the doctrine of the scriptures and the spirit of Elijah would show them both false and take a road between them both. For according to the scriptures, if a man has received the good word of God and tasted of the powers of the world to come, if they shall fall away it is impossible to renew them again, seeing they have crucified the Son of God afresh and put him to an open shame. So there is a possibility of falling away [so that] you could not be renewed again. And the power of Elijah cannot seal against this sin, for this is a reserve made in the seals and power of the priesthood.[16]

Hebrews 6:11–19

[Paul] was careful to press upon them the necessity of continuing on until they, as well as those who inherited the promises,

---

[15]Discourse of 10 March 1844, recorded by James Burgess; *WJS,* 333–34.

[16]Discourse of 10 March 1844, recorded by Wilford Woodruff; *WJS,* 330.

might have the assurance of their salvation confirmed to them by an oath from the mouth of him who could not lie. For that seemed to be the example anciently, and Paul holds it out to his brethren as an object attainable in his day. And why not? I admit that by reading the scriptures of truth, Saints in the days of Paul could learn beyond the power of contradiction that Abraham, Isaac, and Jacob had the promise of eternal life confirmed to them by an oath of the Lord. But that promise or oath was no assurance to them of their salvation. But they could, by walking in the footsteps and continuing in the faith of their fathers, obtain for themselves an oath for confirmation that they were meet to be partakers of the inheritance with the Saints in light.

If the Saints in the days of the apostles were privileged to take the [earlier] Saints for example and lay hold of the same promises and attain to the same exalted privileges of knowing that their names were written in the Lamb's book of life and that they were sealed there as a perpetual memorial before the face of the Most High, will not the same faithfulness, the same purity of heart, and the same faith bring the same assurance of eternal life—and that in the same manner—to the children of men now in this age of the world? I have no doubt but that the holy prophets and apostles and Saints in ancient days were saved in the kingdom of God.[17]

Hebrews 7:1–11

There are two priesthoods spoken of in the scriptures: the Melchizedek and the Aaronic or Levitical. Although there are two priesthoods, yet the Melchizedek Priesthood comprehends the Aaronic or Levitical Priesthood and is the grand head. [It] holds the highest authority which pertains to the priesthood, the keys of the kingdom of God in all ages of the world to the latest

---

[17]Letter to Silas Smith, from Kirtland, Ohio, 26 September 1833; *PWJS*, 299–300.

posterity on the earth, and is the channel through which all knowledge, doctrine, the plan of salvation, and every important matter is revealed from heaven. Its institution was prior to the foundation of this earth, or "the morning stars sang together," or "the sons of God shouted for joy" [Job 38:6–7]. And [it] is the highest and holiest priesthood and is after the order of the Son [of] God, and all other priesthoods are only parts, ramifications, powers, and blessings belonging to the same and are held, controlled, and directed by it.[18]

Paul is here treating three different priesthoods, namely the priesthoods of Aaron, Abraham, and Melchizedek. Abraham's priesthood was of greater power than Levi's, and Melchizedek's was of greater power than that of Abraham. The priesthood of Levi consisted of cursings and carnal commandments, and not of blessings. And if the priesthood of this generation has no more power than that of Levi or Aaron, or of a bishopric, it administers no blessings but cursings. For it was an eye for an eye and a tooth for a tooth. I ask, was there any sealing power attending this priesthood that would admit a man into the presence of God? Oh no.

But Abraham's was a more exalted power or priesthood; he could talk and walk with God. And yet consider how great this man [Melchizedek] was, when even this patriarch Abraham gave a tenth part of all his spoils and then received a blessing under the hands of Melchizedek, even the last law, or a fulness of the law or priesthood, which constituted him a king and priest after the order of Melchizedek, or an endless life. Now if Abraham had been like the sectarian world and would not have received any more revelation, what would have been the consequence? It would have damned him. . . . The Levitical Priesthood was an appendage to the Melchizedek Priesthood, or the whole law of

---

[18]Discourse of 5 October 1840, recorded by Robert B. Thompson; *WJS*, 38–39.

God, when in full force or power in all its parts and bearings on the earth.[19]

The power of the Melchizedek Priesthood is to have the power of "endless lives."[20]

There are three grand principles or orders of priesthood portrayed in this chapter:

First: Levitical, which was never able to administer a blessing, but only to bind heavy burdens which neither they nor their fathers [were] able to bear.

Second: Abraham's patriarchal power, which is the greatest yet experienced in this Church.

Third: that of Melchizedek, who had still greater power, even power of an endless life, of which was our Lord Jesus Christ, which also Abraham obtained by the offering of his son Isaac. [This] was not the power of a prophet, nor apostle, nor patriarch only, but of [a] king and priest to God, to open the windows of heaven and pour out the peace and law of endless life to man. And no man can attain to the joint heirship with Jesus Christ without being administered to by one having the same power and authority of Melchizedek.[21]

Three grand orders of priesthood [are] referred to here.

First: king of Shalom—power and authority over that of Abraham, holding the key and the power of endless life. Angels desire to look into it, but they have set up too many stakes. God cursed the children of Israel because they would not receive the last law from Moses. . . . If a man would attain, he must sacrifice all to attain to the keys of the kingdom of an endless life.

What was the power of Melchizedek? It was not [the]

---

[19]Discourse of 27 August 1843, recorded by James Burgess; *WJS,* 245–46.

[20]Discourse of 27 August 1843, recorded by William Clayton; *WJS,* 247.

[21]Discourse of 27 August 1843, recorded by Franklin D. Richards; *WJS,* 245.

priesthood of Aaron. [Melchizedek was] a king and a priest to the Most High God. [It was] a perfect law of theocracy, holding keys of power and blessings. [He] stood as God to give laws to the people, administering endless lives to the sons and daughters of Adam [by] kingly powers of anointing. . . .

Second priesthood: patriarchal authority. . . .

Third priesthood: Levitical.[22]

Hebrews 7:1

See under Genesis 14:18.

Hebrews 7:3

The priesthood is everlasting, without beginning of days or end of years, without father, mother, and so forth.[23]

[It is] a priesthood which holds the priesthood by right from the eternal Gods, and not by descent from father and mother.[24]

Hebrews 7:20–21, 28

Priests [are] made without an oath, but the priesthood of Melchizedek is by oath and covenant.[25]

Hebrews 11:4

How doth [Abel] yet speak? Why he magnified the priesthood which was conferred upon him and died a righteous man and therefore has become an angel of God by receiving his body

---

[22]Discourse of 27 August 1843, recorded by Willard Richards; *WJS*, 244–45.

[23]Discourse of summer of 1839, recorded in Willard Richards's "Pocket Companion"; *WJS*, 9.

[24]Discourse of 27 August 1843, recorded by Willard Richards; *WJS*, 244.

[25]Discourse of 27 August 1843, recorded by Willard Richards; *WJS*, 245.

from the dead. Therefore, holding still the keys of his dispensation, [he] was sent down from heaven unto Paul to minister consoling words and to commit unto him a knowledge of the mysteries of godliness. And if this was not the case, I would ask, how did Paul know so much about Abel, and why should he talk about his speaking after he was dead? How he spoke after he was dead must be by being sent down out of heaven to administer.[26]

See also under Genesis 4:3–12.

Hebrews 11:8–10

This is why Abraham blessed his posterity: he wanted to bring them into the presence of God. "They looked for a city which hath foundations, whose builder and maker is God."[27]

Hebrews 11:32–35 (11:1–35)

Because faith is wanting, the fruits are not [found]. No man since the world was ever had faith without having something along with it. The ancients "quenched the violence of [fire" and] "escaped the edge of the sword." Women "received their dead," and so forth. By faith the worlds were made. A man who has none of the gifts [of the Spirit] has no faith. He deceives himself if he supposes it. Faith has been wanting not only among the brethren but professed Christendom also, that tongues, and healings, and prophecy, and prophets, and apostles, and all these gifts and blessings have been wanting.[28]

Hebrews 11:35

Now it was evident that there was a better resurrection, or else God would not have revealed it unto Paul. Wherein then can

---

[26]Discourse of 5 October 1840, recorded by Robert B. Thompson; *WJS,* 40.

[27]Discourse of summer of 1839, recorded in Willard Richards's "Pocket Companion"; *WJS,* 9.

[28]Statement of 2 January 1843, recorded by Willard Richards; *PJS,* 3.

it be said, "a better resurrection"? This distinction is made between the doctrine of the actual resurrection and the doctrine of translation. The doctrine of translation obtains deliverance from the tortures and sufferings of the body, but their existence will prolong as to their labors and toils of the ministry before they can enter into so great a rest and glory. But on the other hand, those who were tortured, not accepting deliverance, received an immediate rest from their labors.[29]

Hebrews 11:40

These are principles in relation to the dead and the living that cannot be lightly passed over, as pertaining to our salvation. For their salvation is necessary and essential to our salvation, as Paul says concerning the fathers—that they without us cannot be made perfect—neither can we without our dead be made perfect.[30]

The greatest responsibility that God has laid upon us [is] to seek after our dead. The apostle says, "They without us cannot be made perfect." Now I am speaking of them. I say to you, Paul, you cannot be perfect without us. Those that are gone before and those who come after must be made perfect, and God has made it obligatory to man.[31]

The greatest responsibility laid upon us in this life is in relation to our dead. Paul [said], "They cannot be made perfect without us." For it is necessary that the seals are in our hands to seal our children and our dead for the dispensation of the fulness of times, a dispensation to meet the promises made by Jesus Christ before the foundation of the world for the salvation of man.[32]

See also under Daniel 7:9–14; Malachi 4:5–6.

---

[29]Discourse of 5 October 1840, recorded by Robert B. Thompson; *WJS*, 41–42.

[30]*Times and Seasons*, 1 October 1842, 935; D&C 128:15.

[31]Discourse of 7 April 1844, recorded by Thomas Bullock; *KFD*, 57.

[32]Discourse of 7 April 1844, recorded by Wilford Woodruff; *KFD*, 56.

Hebrews 12:22–24

I will put promises in your hearts that will not leave you, that will seal you up. We may come to the general assembly and church of the Firstborn, [to the] spirits of just men made perfect, and unto Christ. The innumerable company of angels are those that have been resurrected from the dead. The spirits of just men made perfect are those without bodies. It is our privilege to pray for and obtain these things.[33]

And for [what] were they brought thus far? I answer that they came to these personages to learn of the things of God and to hear revealed through them the order and glory of the kingdoms of God.[34]

What could [it] profit us to come unto the spirits of just men but to learn, and come to the knowledge [of the] spirits of the just?[35]

A great many men suppose there is no difference between an angel and a spirit of a just man made perfect, but Paul makes a distinction. He tells us that the Hebrew church had come into the presence of God and angels and to the spirits of just men made perfect. The spirit of a just man made perfect, if he made his appearance, would appear or be enveloped in flaming fire, and no man in this mortal state could endure it. But an angel could come and appear as another man.[36]

The spirits of just men are made ministering servants to those who are sealed unto life eternal. . . . Angels have advanced higher in knowledge and power than spirits.[37]

------

[33]Discourse of summer of 1839, recorded in Willard Richards's "Pocket Companion"; *WJS*, 14.

[34]Discourse of 13 August 1843, recorded by Martha Jane Coray; *WJS*, 240.

[35]Discourse of 13 August 1843, recorded by Willard Richards; *WJS*, 239.

[36]Discourse of 9 October 1843, recorded by James Burgess; *WJS*, 255.

[37]Discourse of 9 October 1843, recorded by Willard Richards; *WJS*, 254.

The Hebrew church came unto the spirits of just men made perfect, and unto an innumerable company of angels, unto God the Father of all, and to Jesus Christ the Mediator of the new covenant. But what they learned has not been and could not have been written. What object was gained by this communication with the spirits of the just and others? It was the established order of the kingdom of God; the keys of power and knowledge were with them to communicate to the Saints, hence the importance of understanding the distinction between the spirits of the just and angels. Spirits can only be revealed in flaming fire, or glory. Angels have advanced farther, their light and glory being tabernacled, and hence [they] appear in bodily shape. . . . The spirits of the just are exalted to a greater and more glorious work, hence they are blessed in departing hence. Enveloped in flaming fire, they are not far from us and know and understand our thoughts, feelings, and motions, and are often pained therewith.[38]

---

[38]Discourse of 9 October 1843, reported in *Times and Seasons,* 15 September 1843, 331.

James

James 1:5

Never did any passage of scripture come with more power to the heart of man than this did at this time to mine. It seemed to enter with great force into every feeling of my heart. I reflected on it again and again, knowing that if any person needed wisdom from God, I did; for how to act I did not know, and unless I could get more wisdom than I then had, I would never know; for the teachers of religion of the different sects understood the same passage of scripture so differently as to destroy all confidence in settling the question by an appeal to the Bible.

At length I came to the conclusion that I must either remain in darkness and confusion, or else I must do as James directs, that is, ask of God. I at length came to the determination to "ask of God," concluding that if he gave wisdom to them that lacked wisdom, and would give liberally, and not upbraid, I might venture.[1]

I had found the testimony of James to be true—that a man who lacked wisdom might ask of God, and obtain, and not be upbraided.[2]

James 3:5–6

Hold your tongues about things of no moment, a little tale will set the world on fire.[3]

James 5:14–15

What is the sign of the healing of the sick? The laying on of hands is the sign or way marked out by James and the custom of

---

[1] 1839 History; *PJS,* 1:271–72; JS–H 1:12–13.

[2] 1839 History; *PJS,* 1:275; JS–H 1:26.

[3] Discourse of 26 May 1842, recorded by Eliza R. Snow; *WJS,* 121.

the ancient Saints as ordered by the Lord. And we should not obtain the blessing by pursuing any other course except the way which God has marked out.[4]

James 5:16

[In reply to the question, "Do you want a wicked man to pray for you?"] Yes. If the fervent, effectual prayer of the righteous availeth much, a wicked man may avail a little when praying for a righteous man. . . . The prayer of the wicked man may do a righteous man good when it does the one who prays no good.[5]

---

[4]Discourse of 20 March 1842, recorded by Wilford Woodruff; *WJS,* 108.

[5]Statement of 24 December 1842, recorded by Willard Richards; *PJS,* 3.

1 Peter

1 Peter 1:23

Being born again comes by the Spirit of God through ordinances.[1]

1 Peter 3:1, 5–7

It is the duty of a husband to love, cherish, and nourish his wife, and cleave unto her and none else. He ought to honor her as himself, and he ought to regard her feelings with tenderness, for she is his flesh and his bone, designed to be an help unto him, both in temporal and spiritual things, one into whose bosom he can pour all his complaints without reserve, who is willing (being designed) to take part of his burden, to soothe and encourage his feelings by her gentle voice.

It is the place of the man to stand at the head of his family and be lord of his own house, not to rule over his wife as a tyrant, neither as one who is fearful or jealous that his wife will get out of her place and prevent him from exercising his authority. It is his duty to be a man of God—for a man of God is a man of wisdom—ready at all times to obtain from the scriptures, the revelations, and from on high, such instructions as are necessary for the edification and salvation of his household.

And on the other hand, it is the duty of the wife to be in subjection to her husband at all times, not as a servant, neither as one who fears a tyrant or a master, but as one who in meekness and the love of God regards the laws and institutions of heaven [and] looks up to her husband for instruction, edification, and comfort.[2]

---

[1]Discourse of summer of 1839, recorded in Willard Richards's "Pocket Companion"; *WJS*, 12.

[2]*Elders' Journal,* August 1838, 61–62.

1 Peter 3:18–19; 4:6

Question: If the Mormon doctrine is true, what has become of all those who have died since the days of the apostles?

Answer: All those who have not had an opportunity of hearing the gospel, and being administered to by an inspired man in the flesh, must have it hereafter, before they can be finally judged.[3]

[There is] a difference between an angel and a ministering spirit. The one [has] a resurrected or translated body with its spirit, ministering to embodied spirits. The other [is] a disembodied spirit, visiting and ministering to disembodied spirits. Jesus Christ became a ministering spirit, while his body lay in the sepulchre, to the spirits in prison, to fulfill an important part of his mission without which he could not have perfected his work or entered into his rest. . . .

There is a way to release the spirit of the dead. That is, by the power and authority of the priesthood, by binding and loosing on earth. This doctrine appears glorious, inasmuch as it exhibits the greatness of divine compassion and benevolence in the extent of the plan of human salvation. This glorious truth is well calculated to enlarge the understanding and to sustain the soul under troubles, difficulties, and distresses. [Suppose] the case of two men, brothers, equally intelligent, learned, virtuous, and lovely, walking in uprightness and in all good conscience so far as they had been able to discern duty from the muddy stream of tradition or from the blotted page of the book of nature. One dies and is buried, having never heard the gospel of reconciliation. To the other the message of salvation is sent. He hears and embraces it and is made the heir of eternal life. Shall the one become a partaker of glory and the other be consigned to hopeless perdition? Is there no chance for his escape? Sectarianism answers, "None! None! None!" Such an idea is worse than atheism. . . .

---

[3]*Elders' Journal,* July 1838, 43.

This doctrine presents in a clear light the wisdom and mercy of God in preparing an ordinance for the salvation of the dead, being baptized by proxy, their names recorded in heaven, and judged according to the deeds done in the body. This doctrine is the burden of the scriptures. Those Saints who neglect it in behalf of their deceased relatives do it at the peril of their own salvation.[4]

Here then we have an account of our Savior preaching to the spirits in prison, to spirits that had been imprisoned from the days of Noah. And what did he preach to them? That they were to stay there? Certainly not. Let his own declaration testify: "He hath sent me to heal the broken-hearted, to preach deliverance to the captives, and recovering of sight to the blind, to set at liberty them that are bruised" [Luke 4:18]. Isaiah has it, "to bring out the prisoners from the prison, and them that sit in darkness from the prison house" [Isa. 42:7]. It is very evident from this that he not only went to preach to them but to deliver, or bring them out of the prison house. . . . Those who were disobedient in the days of Noah were visited by our Savior, who possessed the everlasting Melchizedek Priesthood, and had the gospel preached to them by him in prison. And in order that they might fulfill all the requisitions of God, their living friends were baptized for their dead friends and thus fulfilled the requirements of God.[5]

He knows the situation of both the living and the dead and has made ample provision for their redemption, according to their several circumstances and the laws of the kingdom of God, whether in this world or in the world to come. . . .

When speaking about the blessing pertaining to the gospel and the consequences connected with disobedience to its requirements,

---

[4]Discourse of 3 October 1841, reported in *Times and Seasons,* 15 October 1841, 577–78.

[5]*Times and Seasons,* 15 April 1842, 760–61.

we are frequently asked the question, "What has become of our fathers?" Will they all be damned for not obeying the gospel when they never heard it? Certainly not. But they will possess the same privilege that we here enjoy, through the medium of the everlasting priesthood—which not only administers on earth but in heaven—and the wise dispensations of the great Jehovah.[6]

Let the dead speak forth anthems of eternal praise to the King Immanuel, who hath ordained, before the world was, that which would enable us to redeem them out of their prison; for the prisoners shall go free.[7]

Peter says [Jesus] went and preached to the world of spirits so that they would receive it [and] could have it answered by proxy by those who live on the earth.[8]

All the spirits must either obey the gospel or be damned.[9]

All spirits who have not obeyed the gospel in the flesh must obey the gospel or be damned.[10]

These who will not obey the gospel will go to the world of spirits, there to stay till they have paid the utmost farthing, or till some person pays their debts they owe. Now all those [who] die in the faith go to the prison of spirits to preach to the dead in body, but they are alive in the spirit. And those spirits preach to the spirits, that they may "live according to God in the spirit." And men do minister for them in the flesh. And angels bear the glad tidings to the spirits, and they are made happy by these means. Therefore, those who are baptized for their dead are the saviors on Mt. Zion, and they must receive their washings and

---

[6]*Times and Seasons,* 15 April 1842, 760.

[7]*Times and Seasons,* 1 October 1842, 936; D&C 128:22.

[8]Discourse of 11 June 1843, recorded by Willard Richards; *WJS,* 211.

[9]Discourse of 7 April 1844, recorded by Thomas Bullock; *KFD,* 55.

[10]Discourse of 7 April 1844, recorded by William Clayton; *KFD,* 54.

their anointings for their dead the same as for themselves, until they are connected to the ones in the dispensation before us and trace their lineage to connect the priesthood again.[11]

The sectarians have no charity for me, but I have for them. I intend to send men to prison to preach to them, and this is all on the principle of entering in by water and spirit [John 3:5]. Then you must not only be baptized for them, but they must receive the Holy Ghost by proxy and be sealed by it unto the day of their redemption, as all the other ordinances by proxy. All persons who have been baptized and who have received the Holy Ghost may be baptized for their ancestors or near relatives. God has administrators in the eternal world to release those spirits from prison. The ordinances being administered by proxy upon them, the law is fulfilled.[12]

See also under Isaiah 24:21–22; 1 Corinthians 15:29.

1 Peter 5:5–6

When pride shall fall and every aspiring mind be clothed with humility as with a garment, and selfishness give place to benevolence and charity, and a united determination to live by every word which proceedeth out of the mouth of the Lord is observable, then and not till then can peace, order, and love prevail.[13]

---

[11]Discourse of 12 May 1844, recorded by George Laub; *WJS,* 370.

[12]Discourse of 12 May 1844, recorded by Samuel W. Richards; *WJS,* 372.

[13]Letter to Oliver Granger, from Nauvoo, Illinois, July 1840; *PWJS,* 476.

2 Peter

2 Peter 1

Peter penned the most sublime language of any of the apostles.[1]

2 Peter 1:1–4

The first four verses are the preface to the whole subject.[2]

2 Peter 1:2–11

If you wish to go where God is, you must be like God, or possess the principles which God possesses. For if we are not drawing towards God in principle, we are going from him and drawing towards the Devil. . . . Search your hearts and see if you are like God. I have searched mine and feel to repent of all my sins. . . . As far as we degenerate from God, we descend to the Devil and lose knowledge. And without knowledge we cannot be saved. And while our hearts are filled with evil and we are studying evil, there is no room in our hearts for good or studying good. Is not God good? Yes; then you be good. If he is faithful, then you be faithful. Add to your faith virtue, to your virtue knowledge, and seek for every good thing. . . . A man is saved no faster than he gets knowledge, for if he does not get knowledge, he will be brought into captivity by some evil power in the other world, as evil spirits will have more knowledge and consequently more power than many men who are on the earth. Hence, it needs revelation to assist us and give us knowledge of the things of God.[3]

It is not wisdom that we should have all knowledge at once presented before us, but that we should have a little. Then we can

---

[1]Discourse of 17 May 1843, recorded by William Clayton; *WJS,* 202.

[2]Discourse of 21 May 1843, recorded by James Burgess; *WJS,* 209.

[3]Discourse of 10 April 1842, recorded by Wilford Woodruff; *WJS,* 113–14.

comprehend it. . . . The principle of knowledge is the principle of salvation. The principle can be comprehended, for anyone that cannot get knowledge to be saved will be damned. The principle of salvation is given to us through the knowledge of Jesus Christ.[4]

Notwithstanding the apostle exhorts them to add to their faith virtue, knowledge, temperance, and so forth, yet he exhorts them to make their calling and election sure.[5]

There are three grand keys to unlock the whole subject: First, what is the knowledge of God? Second, what is it to make our calling and election sure? Third and last is how to make our calling and election sure. It is to obtain a promise from God for myself that I shall have eternal life. That is the more sure word of prophecy.[6]

Now brethren, who can explain this? No man but he that has obtained these things in the same way that Peter did. Yet it is so plain and so simple and easy to be understood that when I have shown you the interpretation thereof you will think you have always known it yourselves. These are but hints of those things that were revealed to Peter. And verily, brethren, there are things in the bosom of the Father that have been hid from the foundation of the world that are not known, neither can be, except by direct revelation. The apostle says, " . . . Wherefore the rather, brethren, after all this, give diligence to make your calling and election sure." Knowledge is necessary to life and godliness. Wo unto you priests and divines who preach that knowledge is not necessary unto life and salvation. Take away apostles, and so forth, take away knowledge, and you will find yourselves worthy of the damnation of hell. Knowledge is revelation. Hear, all ye

---

4Discourse of 14 May 1843, recorded by Wilford Woodruff; *WJS,* 200.

5Discourse of 14 May 1843, recorded by Wilford Woodruff; *WJS,* 201.

6Discourse of 21 May 1843, recorded by James Burgess; *WJS,* 209.

brethren, this grand key: knowledge is the power of God unto salvation. . . . There are two keys: one key, knowledge; the other, make your calling and election sure.[7]

[There are] three grand secrets lying in this chapter which no man can dig out, which unlock the whole chapter. What is written are only hints of things which existed in the prophet's mind which are not written concerning eternal glory. I am going to take up this subject by virtue of the knowledge of God in me which I have received from heaven. The opinions of men, so far as I am concerned, are to me as the crackling of the thorns under the pot, or the whistling of the wind. . . .

After having all these qualifications [verses 5–7], he lays this injunction: "But rather make your calling and election sure." After adding all this—virtue, knowledge, and so forth—make your calling and [election] sure. What is the secret? The starting point? "According as his divine power which hath given unto us all things that pertain to life and godliness." How did he obtain all things? Through the knowledge of him who hath called him. There could not anything be given pertaining to life and godliness without knowledge. . . . "After all this, make your calling and election sure." If this injunction would lay largely on those to whom it was spoken, how much more then to them of the nineteenth century?

First key: knowledge is the power of salvation. Second key: make [your] calling and election sure. Third: it is one thing to be on the mount and hear the excellent voice, and another to hear the voice declare to you, "You have a part and lot in the kingdom."[8]

---

[7]Discourse of 21 May 1843, recorded by Martha Jane Coray; *WJS,* 206–8.

[8]Discourse of 21 May 1843, recorded by Willard Richards; *WJS,* 205–6.

2 Peter 1:10–11

St. Peter[9] exhorts us to make our calling and election sure. This is that sealing power spoken of by Paul in other places [Eph. 1:13–14]. [It is] that we may be sealed up unto the day of redemption. This principle ought, in its proper place, to be taught. For God hath not revealed anything to Joseph but what he will make known unto the Twelve. And even the least Saint may know all things as fast as he is able to bear them.[10]

Make your calling and election sure. Go on from grace to grace until you obtain a promise from God for yourselves that you shall have eternal life.[11]

To obtain this sealing is to make our calling and election sure, which we ought to give all diligence to accomplish. There are two sins against which this power does not secure or prevail. They are the sin against the Holy Ghost and shedding of innocent blood, which is equivalent to crucifying the Son of God afresh and putting him to an open shame. Those who do these, it is impossible to renew unto repentance, for they are delivered to the buffetings of Satan until the day of redemptions.[12]

Oh! I beseech you to [go] forward, go forward and make your calling and your election sure.[13]

See also under 2 Peter 1:2–11; 1:16–19.

---

[9]The manuscript reads "Paul." "Peter" was probably intended, because the phrase is found here and not in Paul's writings. The compilers of the *History of the Church* also changed the name to "Peter."

[10]Discourse of 27 June 1839, recorded by Willard Richards; *WJS*, 4.

[11]Discourse of 10 March 1844, recorded by James Burgess; *WJS*, 334.

[12]Discourse of 10 March 1844, recorded by Franklin D. Richards; *WJS*, 335.

[13]Discourse of 12 May 1844, recorded by Thomas Bullock; *WJS*, 368.

2 Peter 1:16–19

Though they had heard the audible voice from heaven bearing testimony that Jesus was the Son of God, yet he says, "We have a more sure word of prophecy; whereunto ye do well that ye take heed, as unto a light shining in a dark place." Now wherein could they have a more sure word of prophecy than to hear the voice of God, saying, "This is my beloved Son"? Now for the secret and grand key. Though they might hear the voice of God and know that Jesus was the Son of God, this would be no evidence that their election and calling were made sure, that they had part with Christ and were joint heirs with him. They then would want that more sure word of prophecy that they were sealed in the heavens and had the promise of eternal life in the kingdom of God. Then, having this promise sealed unto them, it was as an anchor to the soul, sure and steadfast. Though the thunders might roll and lightnings flash and earthquakes bellow and war gather thick around, yet this hope and knowledge would support the soul in every hour of trial, trouble, and tribulation.

Then knowledge through our Lord and Savior Jesus Christ is the grand key that unlocks the glories and mysteries of the kingdom of heaven. . . . I would exhort you to go on and continue to call upon God, until you make your calling and election sure for yourselves by obtaining this more sure word of prophecy. And wait patiently for the promise until you obtain it.[14]

The more sure word of prophecy means a man's knowing that he is sealed up unto eternal life, by revelation and the spirit of prophecy, through the power of the Holy Priesthood.[15]

It is one thing to receive knowledge by the voice of God ("this is my beloved Son," etc.) and another to know that you yourself will be saved. To have a positive promise of your own

---

[14]Discourse of 14 May 1843, recorded by Wilford Woodruff; *WJS,* 201–2.

[15]Discourse of 17 May 1843, recorded by William Clayton; *WJS,* 202; D&C 131:5.

salvation is making your calling and election sure. Namely, the voice of Jesus saying, "My beloved, thou shalt have eternal life." Brethren, never cease struggling until you get this evidence. Take heed both before and after obtaining this more sure word of prophecy.[16]

See also under 2 Peter 1:2–11; 1:10–11.

2 Peter 1:21

We believe that holy men of old spake as they were moved by the Holy Ghost, and that holy men in these days speak by the same principle.[17]

2 Peter 2:1–2

See under Matthew 24:24.

2 Peter 3:10–11

When I contemplate the rapidity with which the great and glorious day of the coming of the Son of Man advances, when he shall come to receive his Saints unto himself, where they shall dwell in his presence and be crowned with glory and immortality, when I consider that soon the heavens are to be shaken and the earth tremble and reel to and fro and that the heavens are to be unfolded as a scroll when it is rolled up, that every mountain and island are to flee away—I cry out in my heart, "What manner of person ought I to be in all holy conversation and godliness!"[18]

---

[16]Discourse of 21 May 1843, recorded by Martha Jane Coray; *WJS,* 208.

[17]*Times and Seasons,* 15 June 1842, 823.

[18]Letter to Moses Nickerson, from Kirtland, Ohio, 19 November 1833; *PWJS,* 304.

1 John

1 John 3:2

How is it that these old apostles should say so much on the subject of the coming of Christ? . . . Can we mistake such language as this? Do we not offer violence to our own good judgment when we deny the Second Coming of the Messiah?[1]

When the Savior appears we shall see that he is a man like unto ourselves. And that same sociality which exists among us here will exist among us there, only it will be coupled with eternal glory, which we do not enjoy now.[2]

When he shall appear we shall see him as he is. We shall see that he is a man like ourselves. And that same sociality which exists among us here will exist among us there, only it will be coupled with eternal glory, which glory we do not now enjoy.[3]

1 John 4:1

It is evident from the apostles' writings that many false spirits existed in their day and had "gone forth into the world," and that it needed intelligence which God alone could impart to detect false spirits and to prove what spirits were of God. The world in general has been grossly ignorant in regard to this one thing, and why should they be otherwise? For "no man knows the things of God, but by the spirit of God" [1 Cor. 2:11]. . . .

"Try the spirits," says John. But who is to do it? The learned, the eloquent, the philosopher, the sage, the divine—all are ignorant.

---

[1]*Evening and Morning Star,* March 1834, 144.

[2]Discourse of 2 April 1843, recorded by William Clayton; *WJS,* 169; see D&C 130:1–2.

[3]Discourse of 2 April 1843, recorded by Willard Richards; *WJS,* 171; see D&C 130:1–2.

. . . "Try the spirits." But what by? Are we to try them by the creeds of men? What preposterous folly, what sheer ignorance, what madness. Try the motions and actions of an eternal being (for I contend that all spirits are such) by a thing that was conceived in ignorance and brought forth in folly—a cobweb of yesterday. Angels would hide their faces, and devils would be ashamed and insulted and would say, "Paul we know, and Jesus we know, but who are ye?" [Acts 19:15]. Let each man or society make a creed and try evil spirits by it, and the Devil would shake his sides. It is all that he would ask, all that he would desire. Yet many of them do this, and hence "many spirits are abroad in the world." One great evil is that men are ignorant of the nature of spirits—their power, laws, government, intelligence, and so forth—and imagine that when there is anything like power, revelation, or vision manifested that it must be of God. . . .

No man can [discern the spirits] without the priesthood and having a knowledge of the laws by which spirits are governed. For as "no man knows the things of God, but by the spirit of God," so no man knows the spirit of the Devil and his power and influence but by possessing intelligence which is more than human and having unfolded through the medium of the priesthood the mysterious operations of his devices—without knowing the "angelic" form, the "sanctified" look and gesture, and the "zeal" that is frequently manifested by him "for the glory of God," together with the "prophetic" spirit, the "gracious" influence, the "godly" appearance, and the "holy" garb which is so characteristic of his proceedings and his mysterious windings. A man must have the discerning of spirits before he can drag into daylight this hellish influence and unfold it unto the world in all its soul-destroying, diabolical, and horrid colors. For nothing is a greater injury to the children of men than to be under the influence of a false spirit when they think they have the spirit of God. Thousands have felt the influence of its terrible power and baneful effects: long pilgrimages have been undertaken, penances endured, and pain, misery, and ruin have followed in their train.

Nations have been convulsed, kingdoms overthrown, provinces laid waste, and blood, carnage, and desolation are the habiliments in which it has been clothed. The Turks, the Hindus, the Jews, the Christians, the Indians, in fact all nations have been deceived, imposed upon, and injured through the mischievous effects of false spirits.

As we have noticed before, the great difficulty lies in the ignorance of the nature of spirits, of the laws by which they are governed and the signs by which they may be known. If it requires the spirit of God to know the things of God, and the spirit of the Devil can only be unmasked through that medium, then it follows as a natural consequence that unless some person or persons have a communication or revelation from God, unfolding to them the operation of spirit, they must eternally remain ignorant of these principles. For I contend that if one man cannot understand these things but by the spirit of God, ten thousand men cannot. It is alike out of the reach of the wisdom of the learned, the tongue of the eloquent, and the power of the mighty. And we shall at last have to come to this conclusion, whatever we may think of revelation, that without it we can neither know nor understand anything of God or the Devil. And however unwilling the world may be to acknowledge this principle, it is evident from the multifarious creeds and notions concerning this matter that they understand nothing of this principle. And it is equally as plain that without a divine communication they must remain in ignorance. The world always mistook false prophets for true ones, and those that were sent of God they considered to be false prophets. And hence they killed, stoned, punished and imprisoned the true prophets, and they had to hide themselves "in deserts, and dens, and caves of the earth" [Heb. 11:38]. And although the most honorable men of the earth, they banished them from their society as vagabonds, whilst they cherished, honored, and supported knaves, vagabonds, hypocrites, impostors, and the basest of men.

A man must have the discerning of spirits, as we before stated, to understand these things. And how is he to obtain this gift if there are no gifts of the Spirit? And how can these gifts be obtained without revelation? . . .

No man nor set of men without the regular constituted authorities, the priesthood, and discerning of spirits can tell true from false spirits. This power they possessed in the apostles' day, but it has departed from the world for ages.[4]

1 John 5:7

See under John 17:9–11.

---

[4]*Times and Seasons,* 1 April 1842, 743–44, 747.

Jude

Jude 1:14–15

[Enoch] appeared unto Jude.[1]

---

[1]Discourse of 5 October 1840, recorded by Robert B. Thompson; *WJS*, 41.

Revelation

Revelation 1–22

This is the first time I have ever taken a text in Revelation, and if the young elders would let such things alone, it would be far better.[1]

I have seldom spoken from the revelations, and I do it now to do away [with] divisions and not that the knowledge is so much needed.[2]

Revelation is one of the plainest books God ever caused to be written.[3]

Revelation 1:1

There is a grand difference and distinction between the visions and figures spoken of by the prophets and those spoken of in the revelations of John. None of the things John saw had any allusion to the scenes of the days of Adam or of Enoch or of Abraham or Jesus, only as far as is plainly represented by John and clearly set forth. John only saw that which was "shortly to come to pass" and that which was yet in futurity. Now I make this declaration, that those things which John saw in heaven had no allusion to anything that had been on the earth, because John says he saw what was "shortly to come to pass" and not what had already transpired. John saw beasts that had to do with things on the earth, but not in past ages. The beasts which he saw had to devour the inhabitants of the earth in days to come. The revelations do not give us to understand anything of the past in relation to the kingdom of God.

---

[1]Discourse of 2 April 1843, recorded by Willard Richards; *WJS,* 171.

[2]Discourse of 8 April 1843, recorded by Willard Richards; *WJS,* 187.

[3]Discourse of 8 April 1843, recorded by Willard Richards; *WJS,* 188.

What John saw and spoke of were things which were in heaven. What the prophets saw and spoke of were things pertaining to the earth.[4]

The things John saw had no allusion to the day of Adam, Enoch, Abraham, or Jesus, only as clearly specified and set forth to John. [He] saw that which was lying in futurity. Revelation 1:1 is [the] key to the whole subject.[5]

Revelation 1:6

It is altogether correct in the translation. . . . The apostles have discovered that there were Gods above. God was the Father of our Lord Jesus Christ. My object was to preach the scripture and preach the doctrine, there being a God above the Father of our Lord Jesus Christ. I am bold to declare I have taught all the strong doctrines publicly, and always stronger than what I preach in private. John was one of the men and the apostles [to] declare they were made kings and priests unto God the Father of our Lord Jesus Christ. It reads just so, hence the doctrine of a plurality of Gods is as prominent in the Bible as any doctrine. It is all over the face of the Bible. It stands beyond the power of controversy. . . . Paul says, "There are gods many, and lords many" [1 Cor. 8:5]. I want to set it in a plain, simple manner. But to us, there is but one God pertaining to us, in all, through all. . . .

No man can limit the bounds, or the eternal existence, of eternal time. Hath he beheld the eternal world? And is he authorized to say that there is only God? He makes himself a fool, and there is an end of his career in knowledge. He cannot obtain all knowledge, for he has sealed up the gate to [it]. . . . In the very beginning there is a plurality of Gods. [It is] beyond the power of refutation. It is a great subject I am dwelling on. . . . The heads of the Gods appointed one God for us. When you take a view of the

---

[4]Discourse of 8 April 1843, recorded by William Clayton; *WJS,* 184–85.

[5]Discourse of 8 April 1843, recorded by Willard Richards; *WJS,* 188.

subject, it sets one free to see all the beauty, holiness, and perfection of the Gods. All I want is to get the simple truth, [the] naked and the whole truth. . . .

I want to reason. I learned it by translating the papyrus now in my house. I learned a testimony concerning Abraham. He reasoned concerning the God of Heaven. In order to do that, said he, "Suppose we have two facts. That supposes that another fact may exist. Two men on the earth, one wiser than the other, would show that another who is wiser than the wisest may exist. Intelligences exist one above another, that there is no end to it" [Abr. 3:16–19]. If Abraham reasoned thus, if Jesus Christ was the Son of God and John discovered that God the Father of Jesus Christ had a father, you may suppose that he had a father also. Where was there ever a son without a father? Where ever did [a] tree or anything spring into existence without a progenitor? Everything comes in this way. Paul says, that which is earthly is in likeness of that which is heavenly [1 Cor. 15:46–48]. Hence if Jesus had a father, can we not believe that he had a father also? . . .

When things that are great are passed over without even a thought, I want to see all, in all its bearings, and hug it to my bosom. I believe all that God ever revealed, and I never hear of a man being damned for believing too much, but they are damned for unbelief.[6]

See also under 1 Corinthians 8:5–6.

Revelation 2:17

There is no angel [who] ministers to this earth [but who] either does belong or has belonged to this earth. And the angels do not reside on a planet like our earth, but they dwell with God, and the planet where he dwells is like crystal, and like a sea of glass before the throne. This is the great urim and thummim whereon all things are manifest—both things past, present, and

---

[6]Discourse of 16 June 1844, recorded by Thomas Bullock; *WJS*, 378–81.

future—and are continually before the Lord. The urim and thummim is a small representation of this globe. The earth, when it is purified, will be made like unto crystal and will be a urim and thummim whereby all things pertaining to an inferior kingdom, or all kingdoms of a lower order, will be manifest to those who dwell on it. And this earth will be with Christ. Then, the white stone mentioned in Revelation 2:17 is the urim and thummim whereby all things pertaining to a higher order of kingdoms, even all kingdoms, will be made known. And a white stone is given to each of those who come into this celestial kingdom, whereon is a new name written which no man knoweth save he that receiveth it. The new name is the key word.[7]

Revelation 3:5

We find [a] promise to individuals living in the church at Sardis which will show something of the blessings held out to the ancients who walked worthily before the Lord. . . . The ancients, though persecuted and afflicted by men, obtained from God promises of such weight and glory that our hearts are often filled with gratitude that we are even permitted to look upon them, while we contemplate that there is no respect of persons in his sight and that "in every nation he that feareth him, and worketh righteousness, is acceptable with him" [Acts 10:34–35]. But . . . we can draw the conclusion that there is to be a day when all will be judged of their works and rewarded according to the same, that those who have kept the faith will be crowned with a crown of righteousness [2 Tim. 4:8], be clothed in white raiment [Rev. 3:5], be admitted to the marriage feast [Rev. 19:7–8], be free from every affliction, and reign with Christ on the earth [Rev. 20:4], where, according to the ancient promise, they will partake of the fruit of the vine new in the glorious kingdom with him [Matt. 26:29; Mark 14:25].

At least we find that such promises were made to the ancient

---

[7]Discourse of 2 April 1843, reported by William Clayton; *WJS,* 169; see D&C 130:5–11.

Saints. And though we cannot claim these promises which were made to the ancients, or that they are our property merely because they were made to them, yet if we are the children of the Most High and are called with the same calling with which they were called and embrace the same covenant that they embraced and are faithful to the testimony of our Lord as they were, we can approach the Father in the name of Christ as they approached him and for ourselves obtain the same promises. These promises, when obtained if ever by us, will not be because Peter, John, and the other apostles, with the churches at Sardis, Pergamos, Philadelphia, and elsewhere, walked in the fear of God and had power and faith to prevail and obtain them. But it will be because we ourselves have faith and approach God in the name of his Son Jesus Christ, even as they did. And when these promises are obtained, they will be promises directly to us or they will do us no good—communicated for our benefit, being our own property (though the gift of God), earned by our own diligence in keeping his commandments and walking uprightly before him. If not, to what end serves the gospel of our Lord Jesus Christ, and why was it ever communicated to us?[8]

Revelation 4:6

The angels do not reside on a planet like this earth, but they reside in the presence of God, on a globe like a sea of glass and fire, [a] sea of glass before the throne, where all things are manifest—past, present, and to come. The place where God resides is a great urim and thummim. This earth, in its sanctified and immortal state, will be a urim and thummim for all things below it in the scale of creation, but not above it.[9]

See also under Revelation 2:17.

---

[8]*Evening and Morning Star,* March 1834, 144.

[9]Discourse of 2 April 1843, recorded by Willard Richards; *WJS,* 171; see D&C 130:6–9.

Revelation 5:6

Probably those were beasts which had lived on another planet than ours.[10]

To have knowledge in relation to the meaning of beasts and heads and horns and other figures made use of in the revelations is not very essential to the elders.[11]

Revelation 5:10

You have got to learn how to be a God yourself and be a king and priest to God, same as all have done, by going from a small capacity to another, from grace to grace, until the resurrection, and sit in everlasting power as they who have gone before.[12]

You have got to learn how to be a God yourself in order to save yourself, to be priests and kings as all Gods have done, by going from a small degree to another, from exaltation to exaltation, until you are able to sit in glory as with those who sit enthroned.[13]

You have got to know how to make yourselves Gods, kings, priests, by going from a small to [a] great capacity, till you are able to dwell in everlasting burning and everlasting power.[14]

You have got to learn how to make yourselves God, king, and priest, by going from a small capacity to a great capacity, to the resurrection of the dead, to dwelling in everlasting burnings.[15]

---

[10]Discourse of 2 April 1843, recorded by Willard Richards; *WJS,* 171.

[11]Discourse of 8 April 1843, recorded by William Clayton; *WJS,* 183.

[12]Discourse of 7 April 1844, recorded by Thomas Bullock; *KFD,* 31.

[13]Discourse of 7 April 1844, recorded by William Clayton; *KFD,* 30.

[14]Discourse of 7 April 1844, recorded by Willard Richards; *KFD,* 30.

[15]Discourse of 7 April 1844, recorded by Wilford Woodruff; *KFD,* 30.

Revelation 5:11–14

John saw the actual beast in heaven, to show to John that that being did actually exist there. When the prophets speak of seeing beasts in their visions, they saw the images—types to represent certain things. And at the same time they received the interpretation as to what those images or types were designed to represent. I make this broad declaration, that where God ever gives a vision of an image, or beast, or figure of any kind, he always holds himself responsible to give a revelation or interpretation of the meaning thereof, otherwise we are not responsible or accountable for our belief in it. Don't be afraid of being damned for not knowing the meaning of a vision or figure where God has not given a revelation or interpretation on the subject.

John saw curious-looking beasts in heaven. He saw every creature that was in heaven—all the beasts, fowls, and fish in heaven, actually there, giving glory to God. I suppose John saw beings there that had been saved from ten thousand times ten thousand earths like this, strange beasts of which we have no conception. All might be seen in heaven. John learned that God glorified himself by saving all that his hands had made, whether beasts, fowl, fishes, or man. Any man who would tell you that this could not be would tell you that the revelations are not true. John heard the words of the beasts giving glory to God and understood them. God, who made the beasts, could understand every language spoken by them. The beasts were intelligent beings and were seen and heard by John praising and glorifying God. The popular religionists of the day say that the beasts spoken of in the revelations represent kingdoms. Very well, on the same principle we can say that the twenty-four elders spoken of represent beasts, for they are all spoken of at the same time and [are] represented as all uniting in the same acts of praise and devotion. . . .

Ye elders of Israel, hearken to my voice. When ye are sent into the world to preach, preach and cry aloud, "Repent ye, for the kingdom of heaven is at hand. Repent and believe the gospel!" Never meddle with the visions of beasts and subjects you do not understand.[16]

Revelation 5:13 proves that John saw beasts in heaven and heard them speak praise to God. [I] do not know what language they speak.[17]

John saw the actual beast itself. It was to let John know that beasts existed there and not to represent figures of things on the earth.

The prophets always had interpretations of their visions, and God always holds himself responsible to give revelations of his visions. If he does it not, we are not responsible. . . .

John saw all beasts in heaven, for I expect he saw the beasts of one thousand forms from ten thousand worlds like this. The grand secret was to tell what was in heaven. God will glorify himself with all these animals. Says one, "I cannot believe in salvation of beasts." I suppose God could understand the beasts in certain worlds. The four beasts were angels there. [I] don't know where they come from. They were intelligent. . . . There is no revelation anywhere to show that the beasts meant any thing but beasts. . . .

O ye elders of Israel, hearken to my voice. When ye are sent into the world to preach, tell them things you are sent to tell. Declare the first principles and let mysteries alone, lest you be overthrown.[18]

Revelation 7:2–3

It means to seal the blessing on their heads, meaning the everlasting covenant, thereby making their calling and election sure. When a seal is put upon the father and mother, it secures

---

[16]Discourse of 8 April 1843, recorded by William Clayton; *WJS*, 185–86.

[17]Discourse of 8 April 1843, recorded by Franklin D. Richards; *WJS*, 190.

[18]Discourse of 8 April 1843, recorded by Willard Richards; *WJS*, 188–89.

their posterity so that they cannot be lost but will be saved by virtue of the covenant of their father.[19]

Now I would ask, Who knows the seal of the living God? Behold the ignorance of the world! A measure of this sealing is to confirm upon their head in common with Elijah the doctrine of election, or the covenant with Abraham, which when a father and mother of a family have entered into, their children who have not transgressed are secured by the seal wherewith the parents have been sealed. And this is the oath of God unto our father Abraham, and this doctrine shall stand forever.[20]

What is the seal spoken of in Revelation 7:3? Find it out if you can. I will not reveal it now but will drop an idea that I have never revealed concerning election connected with the sealing of the servants of God in the fore or top of the head. . . . Covenants, either there or here, must be made in view of eternity. And the covenant sealed on the foreheads of the parents secures the children from falling, that they shall all sit upon thrones as one with the Godhead, joint heirs of God with Jesus Christ. This principle is revealed also through the covenant of Abraham and his children.[21]

Revelation 7:4

See under Revelation 14:1.

Revelation 7:14

[God] will not deliver unless we do prove ourselves faithful to him in the severest trouble. For he that will have his robes

---

[19]Discourse of 13 August 1843, recorded by William Clayton; *WJS,* 242.

[20]Discourse of 13 August 1843, recorded by Martha Jane Coray; *WJS,* 241.

[21]Discourse of 13 August 1843, recorded by Franklin D. Richards; *WJS,* 241.

washed in the blood of the Lamb must come up through great tribulation, even the greatest of all affliction.[22]

Revelation 13:2

The translators have used the term "dragon" for "Devil." . . . There is a mistranslation of the word "dragon" in the second verse. The original word signifies the Devil and not "dragon" as translated. Read chapter 12 verse 9; it there reads, "that old serpent, called the Devil." And it ought to be translated "Devil" in this case, and not "dragon."[23]

Revelation 13:3–4

When the old Devil shall give power to the beast to do all his mighty works, all the world will wonder.[24]

Revelation 14:1

There will be 144,000 saviors on Mount Zion, and with them an innumerable host that no man can number.[25]

Revelation 14:6–7

The angel flying through the midst of heaven: Moroni delivered the Book of Mormon.[26]

The scripture is ready to be fulfilled when great wars,

[22]Letter to W. W. Phelps, John Whitmer, Edward Partridge, Isaac Morley, John Corrill, and Sidney Gilbert, 18 August 1833; *PWJS,* 285.

[23]Discourse of 8 April 1843, recorded by William Clayton; *WJS,* 186–87.

[24]Discourse of 8 April 1843, recorded by Willard Richards; *WJS,* 189.

[25]Discourse of 12 May 1844, recorded by Thomas Bullock; *WJS,* 368.

[26]Discourse of summer of 1839, recorded in Willard Richards's "Pocket Companion"; *WJS,* 13.

famines, pestilence, great distress, judgments, and so forth, are ready to be poured out on the inhabitants of the earth.[27]

See also under Matthew 24:14b.

Revelation 14:13

They rest from their labors for a long time, and yet their work is held in reserve for them, that they are permitted to do the same works after they receive a resurrection for their bodies.[28]

We have again the warning voice sounded in our midst which shows the uncertainty of human life. And in my leisure moments I have meditated upon the subject and asked the question, Why is it that infants, innocent children, are taken away from us, especially those that seem to be most intelligent beings? Answer: This world is a very wicked world. It is a proverb that the world grows weaker and wiser, but if it is the case, the world grows more wicked and corrupt. In the early ages of the world a righteous man—a man of God and intelligence—had a better chance to do good, to be received and believed, than at the present day. But in these days such a man is much opposed and persecuted by most of the inhabitants of the earth, and he has much sorrow to pass through. Hence the Lord takes many away, even in infancy, that they may escape the envy of man, the sorrows and evils of this present world. They were too pure and too lovely to live on earth. Therefore, if rightly considered, instead of mourning we have reason to rejoice, as they are delivered from evil. And we shall soon have them again.[29]

Revelation 15:2

See under Revelation 2:17; 4:6.

---

[27]Discourse of 12 May 1844, recorded by Thomas Bullock; *WJS*, 366–67.

[28]Discourse of 5 October 1840, recorded by Robert B. Thompson; *WJS*, 42.

[29]Discourse of 20 March 1842, recorded by Wilford Woodruff; *WJS*, 106.

Revelation 19:7–8

See under Matthew 22:1–14.

Revelation 19:10

No man is a minister of Jesus Christ without being a prophet. No man can be the minister of Jesus Christ except he has the testimony of Jesus, and this is the spirit of prophecy. Whenever salvation has been administered it has been by testimony.[30]

[The] spirit of prophecy, which is the testimony of Jesus, is necessary to constitute a witness, or a preacher, or a prophet.[31]

God in his superior wisdom has always given his Saints, wherever he had any on the earth, the same spirit, and that spirit, as John says, is the true spirit of prophecy.[32]

Now if any man has the testimony of Jesus, has he not the spirit of prophecy? And if he has the spirit of prophecy, I ask, is he not a prophet? And if a prophet, he can receive revelation. And any man that does not receive revelation for himself must be damned, for the testimony of Jesus is the spirit of prophecy. For Christ says, "Ask and you shall receive" [Matt. 7:7]. And if he happens to receive anything, I ask, will it not be a revelation? And if any man has not the testimony of Jesus or the Spirit of God, "he is none of his" [Rom. 8:9], namely Christ's. And if not his, he must be damned.[33]

See also under Revelation 22:8–9.

---

[30]Discourse of summer of 1839, recorded in Willard Richards's "Pocket Companion"; *WJS,* 10.

[31]Statement of 1 January 1843, recorded by Willard Richards; *PJS,* 3.

[32]*Times and Seasons,* 15 May 1843, 194.

[33]Discourse of 9 July 1843, recorded by James Burgess; *WJS,* 230.

Revelation 20:1–6

Iniquity will hide its hoary head, Satan will be bound, and the works of darkness destroyed. Righteousness will be put to the line and judgment to the plummet, and he that fears the Lord will alone be exalted in that day.[34]

Revelation 20:7–10

The Battle of Gog and Magog is after the Millennium.[35]

Revelation 20:12

You will discover in this quotation that the books were opened; and another book was opened, which was the book of life; but the dead were judged out of those things which were written in the books, according to their works; consequently, the books spoken of must be the books which contained the record of their works, and refer to the records which are kept on the earth. And the book which was the book of life is the record which is kept in heaven.[36]

Revelation 21:2, 9–10

Now we learn from the Book of Mormon the very identical continent and spot of land upon which the New Jerusalem is to stand [3 Ne. 20:22], and it must be caught up, according to the vision of John upon the isle of Patmos. Now many will be disposed to say that this New Jerusalem spoken of is the Jerusalem that was built by the Jews on the eastern continent. But you will see from Revelation 21:2 [that] there was a New Jerusalem coming down from God out of heaven, adorned as a bride for her husband. After this, the Revelator was caught away in the Spirit to a great and high mountain and saw the great and holy city

---

[34]*Times and Seasons*, 15 July 1842, 857.

[35]Statement of 4 March 1843, recorded by Willard Richards; *PJS*, 3.

[36]*Times and Seasons*, 1 October 1842, 934; D&C 128:7.

descending out of heaven from God. Now there are two cities spoken of here. . . . I shall say with brevity that there is a New Jerusalem to be established on this continent, and also that Jerusalem shall be rebuilt on the eastern continent. "Behold, Ether saw the days of Christ, and he spake concerning a New Jerusalem upon this land. And he spake also concerning the house of Israel, and the Jerusalem from whence Lehi should come—after it should be destroyed it should be built up again, a holy city unto the Lord; wherefore, it could not be a new Jerusalem for it had been in a time of old" [Ether 13:4–5].[37]

Revelation 21:3

I discover by this quotation that John upon the isle of Patmos saw the same things concerning the last days which Enoch saw [see Moses 7:62]. But before the tabernacle can be with men, the elect must be gathered from the four quarters of the earth.[38]

Revelation 21:4

After the "little season" [Rev. 20:3] is expired and the earth undergoes its last change and is glorified, then will all the meek inherit the earth, wherein dwelleth righteousness.[39]

Revelation 21:9–10

See under Revelation 21:2, 9–10.

Revelation 22:8–9

The angel that appeared to John on the Isle of Patmos was a translated or resurrected body.[40]

---

[37]*Messenger and Advocate,* November 1835, 210.

[38]*Messenger and Advocate,* November 1835, 209.

[39]Discourse of 16 March 1841, recorded by William P. McIntire; *WJS,* 65.

[40]Discourse of 3 October 1841, reported in *Times and Seasons,* 15 October 1841, 577.

Index